The Path of Intuition

Praise for
The Path of Intuition

I have had the pleasure of knowing Anne since 1987 and have observed her increasingly broad intuitive philosophy and ability. As our world undergoes the broadest changes in known time, we must ask deeper questions to insure our peace of mind and survival. What are the ways we can love ourselves more? How can we make better decisions with intuition? How do we access God for our answers? You will find rich questions and essential answers in *The Path of Intuition: Your Guidebook for Life's Journey.*

—C. Norman Shealy, MD, PhD
founding President, American Holistic Medical Association
author of *Energy Medicine—The Future of Health*

Anne Salisbury is accurate 90% of the time interpreting what the guides convey to her. She is accurate in what she is presenting. She describes it well. Guides, angels, and other energies are also choosing to help her convey the concepts so she can understand them. She has a history of working with guides and angels, and this allows her to trust in what she is receiving. She is truly channeling.

—Barbara Rasor
Emotional Intuitive
Assistant Professor, Holos University Graduate Seminary

As we grow in our understanding of states of consciousness we learn how to get information from and through our higher selves for solving life's problems. We allow "good luck" synchronicity to become the norm. To do this the personality must give up its fears and trust the higher self's bold plunge into what may seem unknown and unpredictable.

Anne Salisbury and Greg Meyerhoff have made the leap of faith to communicate with what they call All That Is. They describe this energy as "that which emanates from Source and is in all things." All That Is tells us, "the connection to Source is what it is all about."

These channelings, or conversations with All That Is, help us remember who we are. They show us how to use our intuition, create what we want in our world, and ultimately return home to Source.

The Path of Intuition helps us connect to the Source within us and inspires us to become more intuitive. It goes a long way in helping us trust our intuition. Through reading the words of All That Is and hearing them reverberate in mind and body, we connect with our own intuition more fully. I highly recommend reading and experiencing the words of All That Is.

—Elmer Green, PhD
founder of Clinical Biofeedback
author of *Beyond Biofeedback*

Anne Salisbury and Greg Meyerhoff have produced a book that guides us to new levels of understanding about intuition. Working through her higher self, Anne shares with us the wisdom of the group, All That Is, with whom she has had two-way communication since she was a child.

To give you some background, six general questions were selected for this book by her doctoral committee at Holos University Graduate Seminary—Norm Shealy, Patricia Norris, Marcia Emery, and Bob Nunley—to be asked of All That Is with follow-up questions asked for clarification. Anne, while in trance, allowed All That Is to speak through her. She let us eavesdrop on her conversations with All That Is as they responded to questions asked by her husband, Greg Meyerhoff. Greg recorded these responses and together they edited them into their present form.

The resulting book, *The Path of Intuition*, is an amazing contribution to the literature on intuition and states of consciousness. It also speaks to fundamental concepts in energy healing and mysticism.

Chairing Anne's doctoral committee was an unsurpassed highlight of my sixty years of academic service. We are delighted to bring this fascinating material to the Academy. It represents a giant step in our search for more effective ways to use our intuition. The channelings of

All That Is—both in *The Path of Intuition* and in private sessions where Greg and I asked questions—are profound, and they changed the way I view the world.

If you have not included intuition as a conscious part of your decision making, you would do well to read Salisbury's books and consult with your own intuition or hers (or some other professional intuitive) on a major decision you have pending. If it works for you, you will reap the benefits of a broader perspective for taking action. If it doesn't work for you, you will at least have the satisfaction of having gained some experience with your "hunches."

If you have included intuition as a conscious part of your decision making, *The Path of Intuition* will empower you to go even deeper and allow your intuitive abilities to blossom more completely.

—Robert Nunley, PhD
Dean of Faculty, Holos University Graduate Seminary
Professor Emeritus of Geography, University of Kansas

It is a distinct pleasure to endorse *The Path of Intuition*. It is both profound in meaning and scope and very user friendly. Many exercises are freely given that enable readers to make as much progress as they desire. I fully intend to utilize these offerings and recommend this book to others.

—Patricia Norris, PhD
past President, Association for Applied
Psychophysiology and Biofeedback
past President, International Society for the Study of
Subtle Energies and Energy Medicine (ISSSEEM)

The central issue for me in *The Path of Intuition* is free will. Do not let the chaos in life diminish your light. Pull back and decide what you want. This is what people need to hear in this chaotic existence. The solutions that All That Is offers through Anne Salisbury are surprising because they hark back to individual choice. Concepts are developed in a multidimensional fashion that bring about uncommon understanding.

The Path of Intuition is incredibly deep. The big lesson that I came away with is that we are truly all related—we are all a manifestation of

All That Is. I am now looking at trees and feeling like I am a part of them. There is a welling up that occurs in me now—it is love and joy.

—John Maling, PhD
former Research Physicist, Stanford University
author of *Have You Ever Held A Mountain?*

Anne Salisbury and Greg Meyerhoff's book, *The Path of Intuition*, arrives at an opportune time. We are already seeing volcanoes awakening, the earth shaking, ice packs melting, and the human race still fighting. To add to this confusion, we are being bombarded with contradictory information from government, religions, and corporations.

Anne Salisbury's channeled information provides a coherent map, a printed GPS, for attunement. Her high spiritual source, All That Is, is brilliant in its simplicity and profound in its implications, affirming the more we find to appreciate, the more energy we have to open to the light of our own Source. And All That Is explains just how to do so. Salisbury's channeled information provides for our awakening.

—Fowler Jones, EdD
Associate Clinical Professor in Psychiatry,
University of Kansas Hospital
President, Psychic Studies Institute

In our Western secular society, intuition is a skill set grossly underused and under appreciated. Using intuition successfully and effectively is not easy. It is a long journey and takes practice. It also requires a couple of good maps in the glove compartment when we get lost. *The Path of Intuition* is a great map—unfold it and use it!

—Donn Hayes, Dipl. Ac., CH
cofounder of OHCO Oriental Herbal Company
founding Vice-President, Acupuncture Association of Colorado

In *The Path of Intuition* Anne taps into the wisdom of All That Is to give us a higher dimensional view of how we can use intuition to change our lives and view of existence. This is life changing information. It helps us love ourselves more and create with more joy. And the timing of this book is significant because, as a people, we need intuition now more than ever.

—Stanley Krippner, PhD
past President, Association for Humanistic Psychology
author of *Demystifying Shamans and their World*

The Path of Intuition as channeled through Anne Salisbury reveals life changing strategies and ideas. This book is truly profound and essential for anyone interested in intuitive development.

This broad perspective takes the reader up to the spiritual level to meet unique metaphors. The reader is guided to embrace concepts that will remain alive long after the pages of the book are closed. I highly recommend this book for anyone who wants to cultivate his/her intuition.

—Marcia Emery, PhD
author of *PowerHunch!, The Intuitive Healer*
and *Dr. Marcie Emery's Intuition Workbook*

In this brilliant book of questions, you are propelled on your own quest for answers to the riddles of life and your life. Tackling these questions is very brave and necessary for living a full life. Anne gives you the template for your quest and opens the door to the process of inquiry and exploration of this great adventure called "you!"

—James Wanless, PhD
creator of *Voyager Tarot* and *Sustain Yourself Cards*
author of *Intuition@Work*

Conversations with All That Is

The Path of Intuition

Your Guidebook for Life's Journey

Anne Salisbury, PhD

Greg Meyerhoff

Foreword by C. Norman Shealy, MD, PhD

founding President, American Holistic Medical Association

The Path of Intuition
Your Guidebook for Life's Journey
By Anne Salisbury, PhD and Greg Meyerhoff
Visit GoIntuition.com

ISBN Paperback: 978-0-9758509-5-4
ISBN eBook: 978-0-9758509-6-1
Library of Congress Control Number: 2013900357

1. Intuition. 2. Spiritual life. 3. Self-actualization. 4. Spirit writings.
I. Salisbury, Anne. II. Meyerhoff, Greg. III. All That Is (Spirit). IV. Title.

Book design by Nick Zelinger
Editing by Phyllis Salisbury / Melanie Mulhall
Book Shepherding by Judith Briles
Published in USA by Lively Spirit, Inc.

)((lively spirit®

Books may be purchased in quantity by contacting the publisher:
Lively Spirit, Inc., P. O. Box 18409, Golden, Colorado 80402, USA
Call 800-375-9703 • Fax 303-474-3071
info@LivelySpirit.com • LivelySpirit.com

Content

Foreword

by C. Norman Shealy, MD, PhD

For the last forty years I have explored the world of intuition, primarily as a tool for diagnosing human diseases. I grew up in a family that was open to the broad world of intuition. My mother frequented a "psychic" just outside our small South Carolina town. Lil Brown was known throughout the state and was consulted by many people, including politicians and police seeking help.

Thus, when I was in my junior year at Duke University, I was quite excited when I was asked by the director of the Duke Players to do a radio skit on the work of Dr. Joseph Banks Rhine, the first professor of parapsychology at a major university. The program was broadcast over campus radio. Although there was no question that Dr. Rhine had proven statistically that psi (the extrasensory phenomena of telepathy, clairvoyance, precognition, and psychokinesis) were scientifically sound, my impression was that rolling dice and intuiting hidden card symbols were not very useful. Meanwhile, I did not pay much attention to my own intuitive "knowing," although in retrospect, I see that I experienced many impressions, and even inventions, as I matured through college, medical school, and the clinical work following my residency training.

Suddenly in 1972, I was thrust back into the relatively obscure world of psychic phenomena with visits to Edgar Cayce's Association for Research and Enlightenment where I had my first past life and out-of-body experiences. Since that time I have had the opportunity to work with a number of gifted intuitives and have also opened channels to my own guides. They have given me downloads that have led to fourteen patents and a number of other useful inventions.

Intuition is the foundation for all creativity in both science and art. Nothing of value would be created without the use of intuition. And just as there are major differences between musicians and artists, so are there major differences between intuitives. Some intuitives have access to a wide variety of information, but most focus on one aspect of information. A few intuitives may excel in business while others specialize in art or a scientific field.

I have had the pleasure of knowing Anne Salisbury since 1987 and have observed her increasingly broad intuitive philosophy and ability. She has been communicating with All That Is, a group consciousness, since she can remember and is grateful for the knowledge they have shared with her over the years. Today, she is asking significant questions of them so that she can share their answers with us.

How do we access God for answers to our deepest questions? I like to believe that we can accomplish that by being still and listening. What are the ways we can love ourselves more? This is perhaps the most critical question of all. Self-esteem is the number one requirement for accessing our intuition and experiencing happiness. I'd say, forgive yourself first and then work toward your ideals and goals.

Why do we need intuition? We need it because it is the key to all creativity and to your higher self. What can we do to increase our intuition? First, we have to learn ways to practice its access. Then we practice, practice, practice. How can we make better decisions with intuition? Once again, practice, listen, and follow the suggestions it offers us.

All That Is, as channeled through Anne, has many more suggestions! And as our world undergoes the broadest changes in known time, we must ask deeper questions and listen to the answers to insure our peace of mind and survival. You will find rich questions and essential answers in *The Path of Intuition: Your Guidebook for Life's Journey.*

Dr. Shealy, a Harvard trained neurosurgeon and the founding president of the American Holistic Medical Association, is one of the world's leading experts in the fields of pain management and alternative forms of treatment. He is a pioneer in the development and use of intuition. He has written scores of books and articles, which have significantly changed the lives of many people, including his highly acclaimed *Energy Medicine: The Future of Health* as well as *The Creation of Health: Merging Traditional Medicine with Intuitive Diagnosis*, which he cowrote with Caroline Myss, PhD.

A Few Words

from Barbara Rasor

Your intuition is never right or wrong—it is just in tune. Intuition is a perception, or an interpretation, of energies. How accurate you are can only be validated by somebody else's subjective perception. That's why it is not a science.

According to my guides, Anne Salisbury is accurate 90% of the time interpreting what the guides convey to her. That is her accuracy rating as an intuitive, or psychic. And, as Norm Shealy has said, "Few in the world are 90% accurate."

There are two things that can cause her to be inaccurate: being tired and feeling that her head is full; and, reading a person who makes the choice not to let go of old patterns in order to heal. Then she is not able to be accurate at all, and I would not be either. Clients must initiate the choice to move forward. Otherwise, as an intuitive, you spin your wheels when you try to help them.

So, Anne is very accurate in what she is presenting. She describes it well. Guides, angels, and other energies are also choosing to help her convey the concepts so she can understand them.

When she is channeling, All That Is shows her an image, and with that in her mind, they start channeling the linear verbiage. She communicates what she is receiving freely without editing or pausing. Anne has a history of working with guides and angels, and this allows her to trust in what she is receiving without waiting for more explanation. She is truly channeling.

You know Anne is channeling when a couple of things happen to her. You will notice that she has that cadence in her voice, which seems to come from a multi-voice group. You will also hear a lot of hesitation or a different kind of tone in her voice. Her sentences will also be more succinct.

When Anne is channeling, she rises above the global human environment and her body feels like it is "home." Her energy frequency increases and shifts, which allows her to bridge the communication gap with All That Is. At different vibrational frequencies, different energies come forward to communicate with her. This allows her to communicate whole new threads of information because she has risen to that level and is allowing her body to go there.

Anne has been taken to the place where All That Is has shown her the essence of God. I have been there, too, and have seen the image of a beautiful fountain with liquid gold droplets. For me, this represents that pure state of energy communication within each of us that connects us to that one power—that one force that it is All That Is.

Anne's channelings involve the process of her going out to where there is a sense of a mass connectedness to that oneness we call God. She is shown the essence of God in a form that we can understand. In biblical times, God appeared in the image of man because that was all that the people could accept. When God said, "You are in my form," he meant our essence was his essence and that we all have God inside of us.

All That Is is a timeless statement. It will invoke something forever. I will now channel a description of All That Is.

"All That Is is the energy of each and every one of you at your base and most perfect frequency. All That Is is the purest form of communication back to the Source, the Source in which you truly and ultimately exist and from which you come. It is that place in which pure love exists in such a form that your minds, your hearts, your very essence of soul can understand, but the form in which you are decreases it by billions. So, to understand All That Is would be overwhelming in the form in which you exist at present. But the form in which you are has that piece within it as a way to return to all that you truly are and to that from which you come."

All That Is helps people remember that they are not alone and that they have within themselves the means to find their own truth. Anne's job is to expand who they are as beings.

Barbara Rasor, assistant professor at Holos University Graduate Seminary, channels about that which Anne channels and in the same manner as Anne. According to Norm Shealy, MD, PhD, founding president of Holos University, who has evaluated intuitives for over thirty years, "Barbara is the best intuitive counselor I have seen." The text above is from a phone conversation in which Barbara answered questions concerning Anne's accuracy and abilities.

Introduction

How would it be if, when faced with a challenging decision, you could completely trust your gut, your intuition? What if you saw your options clearly? What if you were sure that the choices you were making were the right ones? You would feel a tremendous sigh of relief. In those situations, your intuition would be at play and you would be on the path of intuition.

Simply stated, intuition is your access to the oneness we call God, or Source—the Source of All That Is. It is your path to wisdom, wholeness, and personal transformation. It gives you an elevated perspective, enabling you to grasp the path in front of you and make decisions in alignment with your greatest good.

Just as you were given your analytical mind at birth, so were you given your intuition. It is your connection to Source, to all information that you desire. It gives you the ability to be your own expert, to find your own answers and to know that they are the correct ones. When you are "in flow" with your intuition, you are connected to your own wisdom from Source. You make decisions with confidence and ease. You manifest your dreams.

Every single choice you make in life can be meaningful. Think about the last major decision you made. It could have been around entering or leaving a relationship, changing jobs, or moving to a new location. Were you as relaxed and clearheaded in making that decision as you wanted to be?

We often feel frustrated, confused, and critical of ourselves and others when faced with life choices. Perhaps we feel paralyzed with fear that we might make the wrong decision or not be able to make that decision at all. We may not want to hurt anyone, but we are tired of hurting ourselves.

In school we were taught that we needed to gather as much information as possible and listen to the experts in order to make good decisions. "Experts" were supposed to know more than we knew. This rational, logical approach rendered facts—seemingly important facts—but it did not let us "know" the answers that were truly right for us. That sense of knowing is the domain of the intuition.

As children we intuitively knew that life was meant to be fun, fresh, and creative. Having fun was what life was all about. We did not want to just sit in a chair and think. That was what "old" people did, and they looked worse for the mental wear. We wanted to play and laugh. We wanted to live.

In the following pages, we will explore the topic of intuition from the viewpoint of All That Is, a channeled wisdom. You will experience the subtle energy of All That Is as I (Anne) connect and converse with this group consciousness. Through reading and feeling the words spoken by All That Is, you will be able to open to your intuition and know that the subtle energy of Source is within and around you, supporting you in every way. You will be able to feel more alive. You will learn ways to access your intuition and understand why it is so important to use it.

Your intuition is your friend—your best friend—because it is your access to that part of Source with which you can communicate and from which you can receive all the answers you need. You can use your intuition to guide, protect, and inspire you as you consciously choose and create your life's path.

Although some people seem to be born with a greater ability to use their intuition through past life learnings or present life desires, everyone has the potential to develop intuition further. As you practice with your intuition, you can become more confident and increase your potential for being able to channel wisdom with greater clarity. You can increase the significant synchronicities in your life.

Our Hope for You

We envision a society in which intuition is an accepted tool equal in weight to the intellect. Over time, the concept of receiving information from other dimensions will become mainstream. This will bring about a real shift in the way we approach both teaching and learning. Children will be taught to look first within for answers instead of just picking up another book. People will begin to embrace more completely the thought that written words and electronic broadcasts are often biased or comprised of untrue information. This shift in perspective, coupled with the search for truth in every facet of our lives, will have great impact on the human experience. Our hope is that the following dialogue with All That Is will contribute to your shift in consciousness and the subsequent awakening of all those you meet.

Conscious awareness is being challenged to grow at this time. Mental analysis has not given humanity all of the answers we seek. We can benefit from a more balanced approach that combines intellect with intuition. Having a reliable tool, such as intuition that accesses Source knowledge, can help us see through the confusion to find more clarity in our lives.

What is Channeling?

The Path of Intuition: Your Guidebook for Life's Journey is based on channeled material. Channeling is the term we use to describe the accessing of information comprised of universal truth, absolute knowledge, and ultimate reality that is beyond our everyday understanding. Through channeling aspects of All That Is, I (Anne) receive responses to Greg's questions about intuition. These answers make us ponder our universe. They give us food for thought that can lead to monumental wisdom.

Channeling is an art rather than a science. All channelers access information according to their conscious or unconscious interests. The information received from All That Is tends to be esoteric, philosophical, and psychological. It gives you the bigger picture, allowing you to put your life into perspective and enjoy it more.

I connect to a zone of consciousness—cosmic consciousness—that holds far more inspirational information than I normally hold within myself. From this realm, ideas about spirituality are revealed. I receive a stream of information through words, images, feelings, and a sense of knowing. I allow this telepathic connection and communication to continue naturally. It flows as though it has been implanted within me. Sometimes it feels as though my head has just been tuned in to the radio station of All That Is.

This process is challenging because All That Is describes the limitlessness of the universe from their more unlimited perspective and I have to receive this information through my limited human viewpoint. Also, the answers I receive change with any subtle changes in our questions. For example, notice how the answers are dependent upon the questions:

- *Question*: How does a car work?
  Answer: You get in, turn the key, drive.

- *Question*: How do you start a car?
  Answer: You turn the key.

- *Question*: When you turn the key, how does the motor start?
  Answer: The key flips a switch that sends power from the battery to turn on the alternator. That creates enough electricity to fire the spark plugs …

As you will see, continued questioning allows us to go deeper into the heart of the real question. It would be nice to receive simple and concrete answers. Yet, through this process of asking questions repeatedly and slightly differently, we have been able to grasp these concepts more fully and present them to you with more accuracy and in greater depth.

Throughout my relationship with All That Is, I have found that this realm of information, or energy, is available to humanity to help all of us expand into wholeness and love. These questions, when answered, are designed to expand our awareness and love for ourselves and our world.

Introducing All That Is

All That Is is channeled through me, Anne Salisbury. Greg Meyerhoff asks the questions of All That Is and manages the energy space for me while I am in a light trance.

The whole of All That Is is that which emanates from Source and is in all things.

When I reference All That Is later in this text, it refers to the whole of All That Is, the ultimate umbrella that envelops the portion, or group, with whom I am communicating. You could describe them as a group consciousness of nonphysical energy that comes to me from a time and place far from our general experience.

Communicating with All That Is presents me with a broad source of information. They offer me intuitive wisdom beyond my everyday experience. They give me access to the realm of cosmic consciousness— the birthplace of intellectual revelations and artistic inspirations. They refer to themselves in the plural. For example, they say, "And we say to you." They also refer to humans in the plural, so when they say, "you," they mean "you humans."

Introducing Anne Salisbury

I have been interacting with All That Is my whole life. As an intuitive counselor, intuitive business consultant and professional hypnotherapist, I delve into the inner realms to access wisdom. I have a doctorate in psychology, a post-doctorate in theology, and two master's degrees— one in transpersonal psychology and another in business. After leaving the corporate world, I founded the Transpersonal Hypnotherapy Institute in 1990.

Introducing Greg Meyerhoff

Hi, I'm Greg Meyerhoff. I began sitting in meditation a few hours a day when I took up the practice of Transcendental Meditation in the mid-1970s. In the years that followed, I continued to meditate and study metaphysics while becoming successful by applying my intuition in corporate sales. When I married Anne in 2000, we founded Intuitive Advantage, Inc. (which became Go Intuition, Inc.), to help people and businesses make decisions with greater clarity, ease and joy.

Authors' Note

We have kept these channelings as pure as possible. You will notice that All That Is states information in a variety of ways to expand upon the answers to our questions. We have included some of this repeated information to broaden your perspective and deepen your understanding of these teachings.

We encourage you to turn to the Appendix to familiarize yourself with the key words and phrases.

PART ONE

Walking the Path of Intuition

Chapter 1

My Experience As a Channel for All That Is

Before I communicate with this subtle energy of All That Is, I repeat a prayer for protection and connection.

Since I was a child, I have been talking with All That Is in my head. My views of the world and, ultimately, my life have been influenced by my conversations with them. These dialogs have often lasted longer than most conversations I have had with those in the physical realm. I can continue on a topic for days until I feel satisfied with an explanation. Over the years, I have discussed with them aspects about my approach to life and the world around me. They have offered me perspectives that have helped me survive difficult times, and improve my work and my romantic relationships.

People have often asked me, "When you are communicating with All That Is, are you talking to God or to someone or something else?" According to All That Is, they are no different from you and me. They say they are us. They say we are all God and so are they.

Some people cannot understand how I can be talking with God, or more specifically, a vibration of God that is accessible to my questioning. They usually assume that I have to be talking with a deceased loved one or a guide, an alien, an angel, or some other group. But I have never identified All That Is as individuals who are separate from me or separate within their group. Sometimes they show me an image of themselves as a conglomerate or group of beings around a conference table. At other times I can tell that one portion of their energy has come forward with its particular perspective. But none of their members has ever claimed to be a separate entity, and I feel intimately connected to them as a group.

The sense of "knowing ultimate reality" I receive from All That Is is always more expansive than what I experience through using my clairvoyance, or inner sight, in client readings. In other words, I feel an overwhelming sense of "knowing" encompass me that I recognize to be greater than myself when I receive information from All That Is. It urges me to translate the energy of their telepathic messages into words. This urging is accompanied by images, words, physical sensations and emotional feelings such as tears of elation or regret.

When I am with a client and reading clairvoyantly, I primarily see and hear my answers. A little feeling might be added when I need confirmation. When I question a response, the images repeat themselves or unfold further until I fully understand. This process is the same when I talk telepathically with nature, pets, and those who have died. Clients show me images and converse with me in my head. Sometimes, for a brief moment, I may feel physically or emotionally affected during a session. To summarize the differences:

- Clairvoyant, or psychic, readings have a greater sense of being from or within "me."

- Telepathic communications with objects of nature, pets, and people who have died feel like conversations in my head accompanied by visual images that unfold.

- Channeling All That Is feels more expansive in time and space. The vistas are unending. It has a sense of coming from outside of "me." The answers are more impersonal and philosophical. Everything is revealed when I ask. Often, it feels as though I am receiving a download of information from far, far away. Sometimes it feels as though the transmission was initiated even before I was born into this life and I am just now receiving it.

Before I communicate with this subtle energy of All That Is, I repeat a prayer for protection and connection. Quite simply, I ask that the channeling and all those who benefit from it be blessed. Then I ask to connect with All That Is and to the Earth, and I wait to hear confirmation of connection from both entities. I ask to quiet my mind, calm my emotions, and still my body in order to receive from All That Is. There is often a numbing or a tingling at the top of my head. Information then becomes available to me through a sense of "immediate knowing."

Even though all chakras receive information, I seem to access information primarily from my crown chakra, or knowing energy center, when I am communicating with All That Is. This is the seventh chakra on top of the head. By contrast, in clairvoyant readings I mainly see through my sixth chakra, or seeing center, which is between the eyes in the middle of the forehead.

CHAPTER 2

Growing Up with All That Is

As a child, I discovered that questioning authority could cause trouble and make you question yourself. When I was little, I would say things like, "Mommy, why is that woman smiling when she is really being so mean?"

And my mother's response would be, "Be quiet. That isn't nice to say. That is not true."

It was true and I said it. Yet, I was not supposed to see what I intuitively knew to be true. And if I insisted on seeing and knowing things, then I was at least not supposed to acknowledge them.

How was I to be honest? I would be reprimanded if I told a lie, which was actually only referenced as a "fib" or a "story." It seemed that the most important thing in life was to be polite. How could you be honest and polite at the same time? The only solution that I could come up with was to be quiet.

When I was about eight years old, I mentally questioned the correctness of a minister's words about the life of Jesus. While he was talking, I heard a voice inside of my head answer my question. This took me by surprise. "Jesus never said that, or meant that," it said. "Jesus just wants you to love yourself, really love yourself, and all else will be fine."

I sat there for a moment, stunned, and then I turned to my mother and whispered in her ear, "Jesus did not say that." She looked at me, confused. So I repeated myself, thinking I must not have spoken loudly enough to be heard. "Jesus did not say that." With a frown on her face and firmness in her voice, she let me know that I needed to be quiet and listen to the sermon. So I sat quietly in the pew and continued my first memorable conversation with All That Is.

As the years progressed, I wanted to share these amazing conversations with others. I constantly wondered if anyone else was receiving this type of communication. Surely others must be having these conversations in their heads. They felt so natural. To my dismay, I soon discovered that not everyone was doing this. In fact, in querying my family members, I found that there was only one person who accepted the possibility that I could hear voices in my head—my grandmother. She was my favorite relative and best friend.

My grandmother, Madeline, was well educated and brought up as a Unitarian at the turn of the nineteenth century. She was a poet and an admirer of Ralph Waldo Emerson, and she had been a suffragette as a young woman. Her father, my great-grandfather, had been a bold visionary who supported freethinking. He overcame the loss of a leg and an eye to contribute to the early development and beautification of our hometown, Kansas City, Missouri.

Because my sister and I spent two evenings a week at my grandparents' house, my grandmother and I had time to talk about anything and everything. When I told her that my mother disapproved of my challenging the words of the minister, she said, "Jesus was a good man, and we cannot be sure of his words. You can communicate with God in your heart, and I'm sure that Jesus would want you to do that. Why don't you talk to God yourself?"

Before this, no one had ever suggested that I could talk to God myself. I felt supported and validated. My grandmother encouraged me to be inspired through contemplation and nature. When I took her advice, I found myself talking more regularly with All That Is. I proceeded to tap into this realm of illumination and inspiration, write my own poetry, and draw without thinking. Life was good … for a while.

Conversations with my grandmother turned out to be largely limited to the experience of beauty through art and poetry. I, on the other hand, wanted to challenge everything around me to gain a better understanding of my world.

In school, we were encouraged to be creative and intuitive in certain classes, mainly art and English. I excelled in those classes by opening my mind and letting the images and words flow in. It seemed simple, almost like cheating. But the difficulty came when I was faced with science and math. The teachers said I was dyslexic and put me in classes for "dummies." There was nothing anyone could do in those days to make me understand.

Life became even harder with puberty. There was more pressure to be normal, be accepted, look good, and fit in. My head became filled with confusing thoughts, so I shut down my connection with All That Is to simplify my life. In turn, this made me feel conflicted and fuzzy in my head. The world did not make sense.

This absence of mind was not lost on friends. "Earth to Anne!" they called out to me. So, at age fifteen I began to practice Transcendental Meditation to help me focus and raise my dismal grade average. My parents and teachers were thrilled with the results and gave me awards for my new academic achievements.

Sadly, this joy of reconnection with spirit was short-lived because college brought with it the pummeling of peer pressure. This time, I tried harder to shut down my telepathic connection with All That Is, but it was like trying to suppress my own breathing. It couldn't be done. It was like holding my breath for as long as I could, then surrendering to deep gulps of air. I was bulimic, suicidal, and exhausted by confusion.

After I left for college, my mother, through the forced enlightenment of divorce and disease, left the confines of traditional religion and joined the ranks of seekers on the spiritual path. She embraced and experienced the miracles of alternative healing in her newfound freedom. While my parents' divorce gave my mother a sense of freedom, I was feeling less freedom than I'd had in college. I now had to take charge of my future, whether or not I liked it. Having breezed through college as a studio art major, it was now time to become serious. I took a job in fine jewelry sales before taking things even more seriously by returning to school to earn an MBA. Brainstorming in marketing classes was enlivening, but without tutoring, the analysis involved in accounting and statistics would have been my demise.

To prove to myself that I could survive in the analytical world, I submerged my intuition further and proudly took corporate jobs in financial planning and analysis before I shifted to real estate sales and investments. In essence, I had lost my intuitive mind.

By the summer of 1987, at age thirty, I could no longer push the proverbial boulder up the hill in an attempt to be someone I was not. It was too hard to make a living without feeling connected to Source through All That Is. I was screaming inside to find a life path with more meaning.

That July I attended a live channeling event in Kansas City. There I was introduced to a small book on a hypnotherapy process that embraced shamanism and channeling. It advertised a hypnotherapy certification training that would take place that next month. The possibility of combining spirituality and a career as a hypnotherapist gave me the impetus to make a life change. It was time to leave the more analytically oriented world behind and begin the study of the power of the unconscious mind.

A week after this life changing decision, a synchronistic event occurred. That week my mother read a small notice in the newspaper announcing that her doctor from Springfield, Missouri, Norman Shealy, MD, was opening a satellite office in Kansas City. Feeling confident about the changes I was creating for myself, I quickly assumed that he would need a good hypnotherapist on staff. I could be the one. I immediately drove south to meet him for an interview. While I was sitting in his office, he called his medical intuitive, Caroline Myss, for a confirmation before he hired me. She said, "Anne looks like a budding psychotherapist." The term "budding" was appropriate because I had not yet received my hypnotherapy training, let alone training in psychotherapy. With Caroline's blessing, Norm hired me to begin as soon as I had completed my certification in hypnotherapy.

This string of events following my original intuitive decision let me know that I was finally on my life path. My fascination with the vast potential of the unconscious mind eventually lead me to a graduate degree in transpersonal psychology and my founding of the Transpersonal Hypnotherapy Institute. By 1990, I had found a way to call forth intuition in everyone, whether it was through training hypnotherapists to intuit their clients' needs or through sitting with clients and guiding them on their journey into their own inner worlds. This was followed with more training in intuitive skills and advanced degrees in psychology and theology.

CHAPTER 3

Going Public with All That Is

*What are you asking them,
and what are they answering?*

From childhood and into my forties, All That Is was my kindest and most consistent group of friends. They were my confidants because I had learned that it was not safe to speak my mind freely. No matter the situation or my present companions, I could always talk to All That Is. In one sense, they formed a safety net for unreliable friends and, later, disappointing dates. I could even talk to them telepathically if a dinner conversation became challenging.

Then, at age forty-two, things changed for the good. I met my husband-to-be, Greg, who wanted me to confide in him. He wanted to know what I was thinking and feeling. He wanted me to come out of my cave into the light of conversation. He had noticed that I sometimes became silent and "went off" somewhere in my head, and he asked me about it. Others had either not noticed or not challenged me on this. But since Greg had been meditating hours each day since the mid 1970s, I assumed that he, too, was having similar conversations in his head from time to time. So I answered him casually saying, "I'm just talking with a group of beings in my head. I had some questions."

He was shocked. He said he was definitely not having these discussions in his head and he felt left out. He then asked, "Well, what are you asking them, and what are they answering?"

I briefly reviewed what they had just told me, and he became even more intrigued. He wondered if he could ask some questions himself.

I said, "Why not try."

It was at this time that my official, more public, channeling began. Greg told me that I was indeed channeling most of my life, even though the words were only heard in my head. Since college, I had been privately journaling questions and answers through what I knew to be automatic writing and my own form of interactive dream analysis. Greg encouraged me to open up and speak into the recorder because he felt the answers to his questions were significant, at least for him. He thought others might like to hear answers to other questions as well.

Greg judged the process to be important because he had spent years attending weekly channeling sessions while living in New Orleans and Seattle. At the same time, he was also listening to the audios of well-known channeled beings, such as Lazarus and Ramtha. He felt that the information I was bringing forth was more personally meaningful for him.

This support gave me the confidence to come out of my personal shell about All That Is. Since 2004 we have been recording the majority of the channeled sessions, and the information from these sessions has changed our lives. The new and fresh perspectives we have gained have helped us move more quickly through our own issues and grow as human beings.

All That Is has been instrumental in keeping us focused on what we are here to do. According to All That Is, the understanding and use of intuition is important for mankind to perfect. We are all born with this ability, and it is time to activate this potential.

PART TWO

The Path of Intuition

CHAPTER 4

The Big Picture

*We can make choices with the support
and clarity of intuition, or we can
shut it down and travel alone.*

Comment from Anne and Greg: The information in this chapter comes from channeled material, but we have summarized and interpreted it. This information came in response to fundamental questions we had about intuition, creation and our purpose for being. While the essence of the information came from All That Is, it is written from our perspective and gives examples that may help you grasp the concepts. In later chapters we simply give you our questions and the specific answers from the perspective of All That Is.

In the beginning, there was love. Love became curious. It had a thought, and then there was light. Light was born out of the body, or fabric, of love. The fabric of love allowed itself to be the petri dish for light. Light then amassed itself into a nucleus, which we call Source.

Source spun out sparks of light from its nucleus further into the fabric of love, the petri dish, and deposited the sparks there. Time elapsed. After an individual spark of light developed itself enough into a mini nucleus, a portion of the light at Source became interested in it. A portion of light then outstretched itself into the fabric of love to touch that spark and other sparks of light, one by one. This brought more light to the sparks and ignited them.

Thus was birthed new creations, or universes, in the fabric of love. This was the beginning. All That Is was born through this continued outstretching of light from Source.

You could say that out of the body of love was formed an arm of light that outstretched its fingers and brought more light into creation. Out of each finger was born another hand with fingers, and on and on the process continued. This developed into a large family tree of light with Source at the top.

Therefore, you and I are birthed of Source just as we are born of our parents, grandparents, great grandparents, and so on. In this way, everyone and everything is related. You could say that we are made of God because we are created from Source, or a greater God. We are created and we are further creators of our universe. We are children, created by our parents, and we have children, our creations.

We are explorers and travel journalists who volunteer to have experiences and report back to Source.

Here is an illustration describing how we, as children of Source, were created and sent out into the universe to experience life. Let's imagine that Source is living in a small town in Iowa and wonders what it would be like to live in the next town. So Source sends someone (a spark of light) there to see what it is like and has him communicate what he finds there. Then Source wonders what it would be like to live in the next state over, so it sends someone over there to explore. Next, Source sends someone across the ocean, and someone else to the moon, and on and on it goes.

As a culture, we send satellites, probes, and people to the moon to see what is there and collect rocks. We are curious about the possibilities, just as Source is curious about what is in its backyard. We are explorers and travel journalists who volunteer to have experiences and report back to Source. As journalists, we can call in our stories or return home with a slide show. Calling in is like contacting Source with intuition. Returning to share a slide show is more like the universe contracting itself from the outreaches of light back to the nucleus of Source. We can make our full report and stay home for a while.

Why did Source do this? Is this the first time that Source has done this, or has it done this many times before? How long does it take to go out, explore, and report back?

Some of us are now in the process of returning to Source to report in and give our slide show in person. We will then be asked to choose another assignment, or perhaps we will be assigned to one if we are unable to choose for ourselves. We can wonder what the next journey into expansion entails.

Just as sparks of light are sent out by Source to explore its domain, we are excited about discovering what we can create for ourselves. Some adventures are brief. We collect information quickly and move on. Other adventures become tedious and we look for a different challenge to excite us. If we begin to select dangerous adventures to test our limits, we can become detained and this affects our plans for reporting back and returning home.

Imagine that you are an early explorer. Your ship hits a reef, forcing you and your shipmates to swim to the shore of an isolated island. After generations, your descendants forget the nature of your homeland. The truth that was known to the original survivors becomes a myth passed down from generation to generation until the stories are so distorted that they would be unrecognizable to you.

Hundreds of years pass. Then one of your descendants discovers a cave with strange writings and drawings on the walls. These images describe the ship, the crossing, and the shipwreck. The people come to realize that there must be other islands, continents, and cultures of which they are unaware. The stories that they thought were myths must carry some truths.

Now they are curious. They want to see their faraway homeland. They know they must build a vessel and learn to ride the waters in order to return to it. Some people decide that the journey will be too hard, so they choose to stay on the island. They fear the unknown. Others fear that they cannot make the crossing without some miraculous help. These people decide to let the few brave ones make the journey alone.

In the 2000 movie, *Cast Away*, Tom Hanks was stranded on a desert island after his company plane crashed into the ocean. He was there by himself for years, and no one came to his rescue. It was not until he made the effort to build a raft, calculate the winds and tides, and paddle beyond the reef that he was seen by a passing ship and saved. He had to make the effort to get out of his situation before help could come to him.

Through our intuition, Source responds to our requests and feeds us information.

This is similar to our situation today. Many of us came to Earth and became stranded. We became stuck in the mud pond of dense negative thinking and have found it hard to become lighter spirits again. Through ancient texts, we have found clues about our origins. We have received insights from those who have spent years in meditation, those who have stayed in touch with the Earth, and those who have channeled information from subtler realms. Each of these pioneers raised their consciousness, and now they are helping us raise ours so we may be the brave ones who make the journey home. They are showing us how and why we are here on this island called Earth and how we can make it home to Source, or God.

What prevents us from seeing the truth of who we are? What prevents us from growing and changing? What beliefs limit us from moving ahead? What myths are actually true? There are many dimensions of existence beyond ours to be explored.

There is something we can do. When we receive an intuition that helps us to make a personal change and grow, we can take action upon that intuition. We can create something new in our universe. We can help ourselves off of the island of limited thinking and cross the great expanse that leads us home to Source.

Through our intuition, Source responds to our requests and feeds us information. It is then up to us to follow through and act. Once we are willing to make the effort to build the necessary ships, help will appear to escort us home.

Before we take off on any journey of exploration, we are given a lifeline to Source. The tube of light that connects us to Source has within it a combination of life force energy and the energy of intuition. We need both to survive. The light of life force energy supports our bodies, and the light of intuition supports our minds with all the information we need as ignited sparks of light, or humans.

We have the choice to remain healthy and vital on our journey, or we can create sickness and disease. We can make choices with the support and clarity of intuition, or we can shut it down and travel alone. Both life force energy and intuition can be reduced or completely shut off by us if we so choose. Sometimes these choices are made consciously, and other times they are made through unconscious beliefs or programs.

Intuition is key. It allows us to communicate with our higher selves and Source so we can both request and receive the information we desire. We need our intuition to be flowing to receive assistance and direction.

There is something we can do. When we receive an intuition that helps us to make a personal change and grow, we can take action upon that intuition. We can create something new in our universe.

CHAPTER 5

The Light and Creating

To create, you must first remember
that you are God, a creator.

Comment from Anne and Greg: The questions from here forward are asked by Greg, after Anne enters a meditative state. The responses are given by All That Is, a group of nonphysical beings who speak through Anne. They want us to fully embrace this material, so they often repeat themselves, making only subtle differences in their answers.

When All That Is refer to "All That Is," they mean the whole of All That Is, the ultimate umbrella that envelops the group with whom I am communicating. When they say "you," they are speaking to all of us. When they say "Source," they are referring to the greater, or ultimate, God. They say we are made of God, so when they say "you are God," they mean that we humans are all Gods, creators in our individual realms.

Question: What is the light?

The light is an information pattern, which you could see as a tube of information, that descends into your world. It connects you to Source, or the greater God, and it reminds you of who you are. It holds within it everything you need to know in order to function.

The light goes in two directions, both to and from Source. Source comes down with light to ignite the sparks of light that are ready for it, and it then continues to feed those sparks with the light of intuition and life force energy. Light also goes back to Source with requests for intuition.

When you follow the light up the so-called tube, beam, or column to Source, you see that it is composed of many particles. These particles remind you that you are one with God, or Source, because each particle has within it the connection to Source. Each particle is separate, yet whole in itself, while being a part of you and a part of the whole.

When you feel yourself filled with the light, you can know all things, for nothing is separate from you. This memory pattern of who you are as God in your realm, world, or universe allows you to be anything you desire. It reminds you that you have the ability to create anything. But to create, you must first remember that you are God, a creator.

Next, you must have confidence in your creating. Your confidence in creating depends on how much creating you have done in previous experiences or lifetimes. As your confidence level increases, you can create more and more. You can eventually move more quickly from first grade to college.

Some children are considered to be geniuses because they remember that they are God at an early age. Their memory pattern is ignited in the light, and they remember they are whole. So they can skip ahead a few grades with ease. Others are unsure about whether they have learned something before, so they slow themselves down by their uncertainty. You want to ensure that you are ready to move ahead. You want the experience of practice to help you become sure of yourself.

Question: It seems as though some people are more connected to the light than others. Can a person exist without the light?

If the light does not extend into your world, or at least a portion of your world, then life cannot exist there. Without the light, it becomes "lights out," so to say. There is no existence, no participation in your world.

The pattern of development is set up in your world to allow for anything to exist that has been touched by the light, by the fingers of

Source. This means that once the connection has been made, existence may be experienced. However, after the spark of light has been ignited there must be enough energy in the pattern of light particles to bring forth a flowing stream of that light. The light can only descend more fully if it finds a sufficient amount of love. Love is always required to enfold the light.

You could imagine a tube of light, or beam, that naturally wants to enter a bouncing beach ball. The desire, or request, for the light to descend must be within the beach ball and the tube in order for it to descend. To receive the light, love must be present within the beach ball. If love is not present, the light tube stops short of entering into that beach ball and the beach ball does not experience the light even though it is so very close.

As a being, you must desire, request, and receive the light. The desire to be in this existence exists within you in the light at Source. You, as the receptacle or being that receives this experience of light, are set up to receive it in love.

This memory pattern of who you are as God allows you to be anything you desire.

CHAPTER 6

What Is Intuition?

*Intuition is both the tube and the
light of information that flows
through the tube from Source to feed you.*

Question: What is intuition?

Intuition is your access to information that is available from Source, or God the ultimate creator in your universe. It is your direct connection to a stream of answers that are available to you when you ask. Think of it as a type of tube or beam or column of light that descends into your world and connects you to Source. This so-called tube brings you a "cloud" or stream of information that you can translate into meanings for you. When you ask a question, it goes up your tube of light to your higher self, your full self, and then to Source, and the answer is returned to you through that same tube. The goal is to ask questions, listen, and wait for the response.

*Your intuition feeds you all the information
you need to maintain your world.*

Intuition is both the tube and the light of information that flows through the tube from Source to feed you. More specifically, your life force energy and intuition come down the tube as a stream of light particles that fill you as the receptacle, or receiving device. Your connection to Source, as well as your ability to maintain that connection, is a part of your system. You maintain this activity, or flow, through the love you have for yourself. As long as you love yourself and maintain your vehicle, or body, you will have an experience of being God in the physical realm.

Experiencing yourself as God, a creator, is your purpose for being here.

Your experience of being God, creator in your realm, is allowed and maintained through your connection to Source. Intuition issues meaning to life and holds for you the original idea of who you are. You gain purpose through understanding who you are, and that definition is given to you by your intuition when you ask.

Experiencing yourself as God, a creator, is your purpose for being here. By being the creator in your reality, you expand and grow. Because you are only partially present in this reality, or dimension, your ability to communicate with your full self and Source is paramount for your survival and maintenance in this world. This is why intuition is so important. It connects you to Source. It allows you to communicate from your limited incarnated physical self through your higher self to your full self and Source. Your higher self is that part of you that is partially incarnated, whereas your full self is all of who you are.

Your intuition feeds you all the information you need to maintain your world. All answers are given to your questions. Nothing is held back unless it is inappropriate for you to know it at that time. The meaning you ascribe to the answers may be pure or may be polluted depending upon the filters or beliefs with which you translate the information.

The difficulty comes when you doubt your world and yourself as God, creator in your realm. This reduces your access to intuition. When you love and appreciate yourself less, there is less love in the universe to hold you. You must personally love yourself to bring forward the love of the universe that supports and holds you in place in your world. This love you have for yourself creates the space for you to create.

The tube retracts slightly when you distrust yourself, and the degree to which it retracts depends upon how many times you have distrusted yourself. In order for information to come through the tube, it must be connected to Source.

You must remember that you are God. Then access your tube of light, which holds within it your intuition, to maintain your world and create your desires. It is up to you, as the God of your realm, to make these choices to do these things.

You are beings of light. Source feeds light to you. You are always connected to Source as an individual experience of Source, or God, while you are in this reality. If a disconnection is made, either through your choice or some surprise happening, then your light is extinguished at that location in the fabric of love and your tube is instantly withdrawn. That terminates your present experience.

Question: Why do we need intuition?

Your being—your experience of life on this planet—requires connection to the Source of All That Is in order to survive. The mechanism of intuition feeds you with all you need to know. This energy pattern that descends from Source allows you to be in this universe you call "life" and create however you please.

Your intuition is available to help you move ahead. It reminds you that you are God, creator in your realm. It accesses Source and brings forth light, which has within it life force energy and intuition, so that you may create. It is the homing device that ultimately leads you home to Source.

The goal is to ask questions, listen, and wait for the response.

CHAPTER 7

The Story Behind Wholeness and Separation

*When you desire to be more intuitive,
you automatically increase your connection
to Source, and intuition flows more fully.*

Question: Are we separate creators or are we a part of the whole?

If you look to the string of energy above your head, you will see that you are connected to Source. Without this connection, you are nonexistent. Those who say that they are fine being separate from Source may look as though they are lacking energy—a bit dried up. This is because their connection to Source is lessened by their desire to be wholly functional without the resources of, or connection to, Source.

You could see intuition as a stream of light that descends from the source of light. This stream is part of the whole of light, and it is the creating device that you use to operate in your world. You are both whole and separate. Truly, you are a part of the light and, as such, you are whole. While you feel somewhat separate in this Earth experience, any separation is an illusion.

When you desire to be more intuitive, you automatically increase your connection to Source, and intuition flows more fully. You expand your desire for the light and it is given to you. It is that simple. You could say that it is a matter of "ask and it is given."

When you desire to function on your own as yourself, you decrease the light that enters your system. This is a choice that everyone has, a choice you can always make. If you decrease your light, your ability to function as God is diminished. This is because the light must enter your system for you to be fully functional as God, or creator, in your realm. Wherever there is less light, there is less functionality.

Love holds you and encompasses you in your world so you can receive, accept, and prefer the light to the absence of light. Love is like a blanket that wraps around you in such a way that you appreciate yourself more. It is a part of your experience. When you love yourself more, your ability to receive light and intuition is increased.

The light can grow when you are encompassed by love. When there is more of you present, when you are fully you, there is more love. Then you are "in love," which is a state of wholeness that is fully receptive. To be filled with light, you must already be in a state of love. To experience love, you must already be filled with a base of light. It is the case of the chicken and the egg.

The experience of separation is granted for each life experience so you may learn who you are as God, as creator, in your realm.

When you love yourself and accept the light, your communication with All That Is is granted as fully functional. This is because there are no places where you are not when you are filled with love and are therefore whole.

There are many ways to describe intuition. It descends in the light with life force energy into your being that is held in love, thereby giving you the ability to continue to grow and communicate with all beings. Let us say that you are walking down the street and you decide to use your intuitive abilities to talk with a dog that is sitting in the grass. You communicate with this animal telepathically and he communicates back to you. This is natural for those who continually use their intuition.

The dog is a part of you because he is in your universe, your realm. The dog is not separate from you. No separations exist in your world. The connection between the two of you is a part of your being. Your ability to see and understand all things is granted through your connection to the light. You can see All That Is in the universe when you are connected to the light.

You may say, "Oh, but in our world we are separate, we are each creators, we are gods."

And we say to you, "True. Very much so." You are separate in that you create in your own realm. But in the bigger picture, you are whole. The separation, the experience of also being separate, is granted so you can realize the beginnings and endings for your individual creations.

Once you know that you are whole, pure, and one, you no longer feel separate. It is a dynamic that may appear to be confusing, yet it is the setup or design.

You work within your system of energy to create those things you desire to experience. This is your realm, your holographic existence, so to say. And when you are complete with your existence, you simply "turn out the lights." In other words, you extend your energy back to Source and deplete your energy in this existence of separation. You are complete with this particular experience and then pass into a different experience.

You may say, "Oh, but how can I be both separate and whole?"

And we say to you, "The experience of separation is granted for each life experience so you may learn who you are as God, as creator, in your realm." You must have practice sessions to become good at it. These practice sessions are granted to you through your experience of separation.

This is why, we repeat, you are creators in your realm. Once you know that you are whole, pure, and one, you no longer feel separate. It is a dynamic that may appear to be contradictory or confusing, yet it is the setup or design.

CHAPTER 8

How to Be More Intuitive by Loving Yourself

Desire ignites the spark of light in your world.

Question: Why is love so important?

The potential "you" is a pattern of energy, or configuration of light particles, that desires to receive more light. If this potential "you" has not already loved itself enough to create joy within it to welcome and receive the light, the light will hold back. Also, if you, as a pattern of energy, feel unwilling to hold yourself in love, the love dissipates. You then experience sadness, remorse, loneliness, or some other form of lack of love. This pattern keeps replicating itself and leaves you in a state of even less love. This means that you are even less able to receive the light.

As this lack experiences itself over and over again in your system, it becomes disease. This dis-ease is a dysfunction in your energy pattern. It has no holding pattern for the light. As it grows, it rejects the light more and more. Therefore, it takes an act of intensity, or what you could call "prayer," to change the energy pattern to be able to receive the light.

The light particles, which have become a dim mass through the state of lack, must be separated so that they are no longer attaching to one another. Then the light can descend within and among the particles.

Your universe is set up, or designed, under the guiding principle that you ask and receive—you function, or create, by asking for what you want and receiving it. The light must know that you fully want to receive what you have asked for to fully descend from Source. If it does not feel loved, it halts in its tracks.

You may say, "Oh, it is unfair for the light to descend just so far and then stop before giving me what I desire."

And we say to you, "This process is a fully functioning portion of your universe, of your way of being." You could say that it is the law of the universe for the light to descend only when the receptacle is ready. The receptacle is not ready when it is functioning as a god who has forgotten itself.

The mechanism that is designed for descending requires that the device, which has been planted in your world for receiving, open its heart fully in order to receive. This device is you, as a pattern of energy, which you, as a spirit, observe in your world.

The abundance of light is the powering device that allows you to move ahead.

Imagine you, as full self or spirit, looking out into the universe and saying, "Oh, look! There is a spark of light. I am that spark of light. I am there in my universe. I think I will go play with that part of me that already exists in the world." You then descend in the light as an energy pattern because you are attracted to participating in the world as a human being. You are excited when you arrive as the light and touch that spark of light that is already in existence in your world. You say to the streaming light, "I am here! I am here! I am ready to fully function in this world. Give me my human attire so that I may exist and become a human. I can hardly wait for this experience to begin. Give me my human outfit and let me play!"

This desire ignites the spark of light in your world. The spark then functions through the love that you have for it. You could say that you brought forward both the love and the light. You remembered you were

God through this whole experience and, therefore, you fully activated your world.

Here is a different example. Imagine looking out into the universe, which is you, and saying, "Oh, look! There I am as a spark of light in my world. That spark is ready for me to experience life as a human. I think I shall go there and have that experience." So you begin to descend in the light, but as you get closer and closer to that spark, or particle, of light already in existence in the world, you begin to have doubts. You begin to wonder if this human experience is truly right for you.

When you touch the spark of light, you start feeling lonely and separated from All That Is. When you turn around from that place of existence to call in more of your light, your call to the universe is weak. Your call lacks commitment and conviction for being on that human path. The light that is descending then halts itself in its tracks and wonders if you are sincere.

If you are not completely committed to the experience, then the light can no longer exist for you. This is what occurs with beings who first desire to be here but then decide to reconsider once they experience the realm of existence as humans. They blink out, or die, or are not fully born in the first place.

They can then sit in the light for a while longer until they decide what they would like to do. As they observe human experience, they can decide once again whether to participate. One of them might say, "I see a baseball game going on down there. I would like to play in that. Boy, would I ever like to play in that game." The light will then descend, bringing that desire to the spark of light that has been in existence for so long, calling that individual to another experience.

You become fully functional and create in your world when there is desire and love for the experience. You must have these two things to remain. If you do not love the experience after you have fully descended into this world, you will find a way to leave. When you retract love, the light begins to pull back. The light only fully exists when there is the full experience of love.

You cannot create fully when there is less light. The abundance of light is the powering device that allows you to move ahead. When depression, anxiety, or stress enters your world, your light dims, for it is pulling itself out.

Question: How can you be more intuitive through loving yourself?

You are a part of the vehicle that experiences your world as Source. You are connected to Source through your intuition, and intuition is at the core of your being. Being intuitive is being who you are. Not being intuitive is not being fully functional. To fully function, you must love, appreciate and see goodness in yourself. Then you can receive the goodness of the universe.

By fully loving yourself, you complete your experience in this world. You experience yourself as whole to make it to the next step. And the next step is revealed to you when you are ready.

You become fully functional and create in your world when there is desire and love for the experience.

CHAPTER 9

Trusting Your Gut

Both intuition and instinct are a part of your
informational system that is connected to Source.

Question: What does it mean to "trust your gut"?
Doesn't intuition come through the light into your head?

The light of intuition emanates throughout your body. When you trust your gut, you acknowledge that your body has received an intuition. When the light of truth extends down into your gut, your bones, or another area of your body, your reactions tell you whether something is right or wrong in your world.

When your body feels truth, it feels calm and at ease. There is a reverberation in your body if something rings true. Your body can acknowledge truth when you have requested to know something through your intuition.

Stand tall and straight and let the light of intuition bring information through your whole being. Allow the light to continue moving down through your legs and your feet to ground yourself to the Earth. You can feel and know everything through your body and mind once you are activated.

Question: How does intuition differ from "fight or flight"
body instincts?

It does not. Instincts are a part of your information system, as is your intuition. Both involve activating yourself as a system for information gathering purposes. You can receive information any way you like—through your body or through your mind. Both intuition and instinct are a part of your informational system that is connected to Source.

Your intuition is your guidance from Source. It is your connection to All That Is. Because of that, your walk is never alone. All of your activities are predicated upon your being connected to the whole and, as such, you participate in your world as an expression of the whole.

You could say that instinct is the simpler aspect of you that communicates with the whole you. It is the survival mechanism that brings information through your body to keep you alive and well. Instincts are the trigger mechanisms that alert you in times of danger.

Question: How do you differentiate between the fear that is a message from your intuition and the fear that is based in beliefs or old programming?

You experience them differently. The fear that is a message from your intuition alerts you to the facts of the situation. It feels pure and simple. The fear that is based in beliefs or programming is impure and complicated.

To break free of unwanted beliefs, you must first acknowledge that they imprison you. Your beliefs and assumptions can misguide you. They keep you from hearing your intuition. When you listen to your beliefs and ignore your intuition, you become less and less able to access the light and, ultimately, less able to access your intuition.

Ask the light of intuition to return to your system and shed light on any beliefs, assumptions, and misunderstandings that you might hold incorrectly within you. Know that the fears you have created for yourself are possibly false. They originated in the lack of love. By cleaning out old habits of thinking, you give yourself the space to create anew.

When you were filled with misunderstandings, you created an unwhole world. This gave you something to complain about. Now you can move beyond these misunderstandings and experience yourself as God, creator of your own choosing.

Many fearful people in your world have unknowingly used fear to hold themselves down. In the long run, everyone can see the light and move ahead because the desire to grow is part of your nature. It is simply a matter of time. So be gentle with those who do not desire to grow. They are resisting the light. They have loved themselves less over time. They know no better. Eventually, they will see that love conquers all, for love allows you to be yourself.

Eventually, you recognize that fighting others, yourself, and your beliefs interferes with your growth. It requires your time and energy. Love of self conquers all. As you love yourself more, others will allow themselves to be less fearful and more in a state of love in your presence. Then they may awaken and the light can return to them as well.

Question: It seems as though fear is being used to control people. How do we avoid that?

You do not. You laugh it off and let that reality be. Walk to the side of it. Know it is not real for you. Know that it can affect you only if you allow it to do so. Why not wrap yourself in the fabric of love? Through love, you create your world. Through fear, everything can crumble because the light is minimized when there is insufficient love.

If others play the game of fear and use it to manipulate, they will eventually be manipulated themselves. Once you enter such a game, you will play both roles, the manipulated and the manipulator. It is only by acknowledging that the game is in play and by stepping to the sidelines that you have true control over yourself.

Assuming that someone has control over you is a fallacy. When you entered this life you asked to be an actor in the play. If you felt fear you said, "Please give me the script for the victim whose toys are taken from him. I would like to play that role." After you played the role of victim to your satisfaction, you revolted, switched roles, and took revenge. You forgot that it was a game and that you were God, creator and experiencer of the game.

Remember, all the toys in the universe are available to you in any game you play. All you have to do is stop playing for a moment and look around you. You can put down the script for the control game and walk away with a smile. You can let someone else take the role of victim and manipulator and watch the game from a distance. Then you are fine.

Question: Can you depend upon your intuition to survive?

If you hold on to intuition—or anything—so tightly that you make it your god, you fall into the trap of asking another to rescue you. You are depending on another for your survival. Then you are not your own god.

If you believe that you cannot survive without your intuition and you fear that your intuition may withdraw itself from your reality, you are actually asking it to retract. Your fear has become your belief. May we suggest that you appreciate the tube of light that is there for you. Assume that it brings you your intuition whenever you desire it. You do not have to grasp it and hold tightly. Simply be yourself and all you desire will be yours.

Through love, you create your world.
Through fear, everything can crumble.

CHAPTER 10

The Mechanics of Intuition

*The universe hears you and brings you
the results you desire.*

Question: What is the relationship between synchronicities and intuition?

Synchronicities are those events that let you know you are connected to All That Is and Source. They are the reminders to you that you are the creator in your world—you are your own God, and you create those events you desire.

Things can be simple and easy when you desire them to be so. When you have cleaned out old beliefs and assumptions, your intentions can be heard at Source. Source can then respond by issuing responses to your requests and you can identify those responses. Your intuition is functioning and your synchronicities confirm that.

For example, have you ever wanted to reach someone but could not find her phone number, and then you went to the store and unexpectedly saw her there? This is a synchronicity because it is unexpected, yet appreciated. The more you appreciate your synchronicities, the more they will abound in your world.

Either at a conscious or an unconscious level, you put out a request to the universe to have something occur. The universe hears you and brings you the results you desire. It could be as simple as questioning whether you should do an inconsequential this or that, and the synchronicity lets you know which direction to take. This is proof that you are in flow with your universe.

To experience synchronicities you must do a couple of things:

- First, to avoid polluting your requests, you must insure that your tube of light is free enough of unintentionally held beliefs. Such pollution can either alter the meaning of your requests or entirely block them from reaching Source.

- Second, your tube of light must be clean enough to receive intuitions that you will recognize as your requests being answered.

You may say, "Oh, but some people who appear to be very unclean in the use of their intuition have synchronicities."

And we say to you, "They have an area in their lives where they are clean and can receive." You only have to be clean in the area that matters for that synchronicity. Also, if there are more than just you involved in a synchronistic event, only the one requesting it needs to be clean enough to receive the information.

Question: How does it work when you see someone at the grocery store because that is your desire, but it is not his desire to see you?

You put out the request, it goes up your tube of light, and the universe responds by bringing that person into your realm of experience. The universe brings that person to you whether or not he is aware of it. However, if he does not want to see you, whether or not the meeting occurs will depend on whose desire is stronger.

In another example, someone could request information and you are the most likely one to give her what she needs. So you are brought into her proximity to benefit her. There is a lot of this tit-for-tat in the universe.

If you help someone today, the likelihood is that someone else will help you tomorrow. When you love yourself today, you set up your energy system to be friendly to yourself and others tomorrow. You can see yourself as a cooperative part of the whole. The kinder you are to yourself, the kinder you are to others and, naturally, the kinder they are to you. It is a joyous collaborative effort that moves everyone ahead.

Question: There have been times when we have had synchronicities that we did not request. For example, we had the urge to exit the freeway early on one occasion only to find out later that we had missed an accident up ahead. This was not a conscious request. What was this?

Whether or not you were conscious of it, you put out a strong request to the universe to be safe and to have the trip go smoothly. That is the bell that you rang loudly and constantly so that the universe would hear you. Intuitions are brought to you to keep you safe and in flow.

Many hold the belief that Murphy's Law is continuously in effect, that "if anything can go wrong, it will." When this belief is sent out into the universe, it boomerangs back to you. This belief will be reinforced whenever the unconscious request for lack of safety and lack of ease has been fulfilled. People with this belief will end up sitting in traffic behind every accident on the road. Sometimes they are unfortunate enough to be involved in the accidents themselves. This is just the kind of evidence that you are granted when you believe in negative situations.

So if you find that you are sitting in an unusual number of traffic jams, you might want to reflect on your beliefs about road traffic. Write a list of all of your beliefs. Look at them and decide if they are appropriate for you at this time. If they are not, decide what you would like to believe instead and send that request up your tube of intuition.

Why not have a safe, easy, and enjoyable life? It is important to contemplate your beliefs. This contemplation and clear decision gives your higher self a greater understanding of what you want and also gives it easier access to you. When your mind is calm and clear, it opens the channels of communication.

Give yourself time to reflect on a regular basis and you will notice many benefits. If you have asked to expand your awareness and traffic jams are the only times you have to quiet your mind and reflect, then traffic jams will be introduced into your reality. But if you desire to do things more easily, you can agree to communicate with your higher self in other more quiet moments, such as during intentional meditations or when journaling your thoughts.

Question: Sometimes when we make a request, what comes back is in a different form from the one we expected. Can you explain that?

When you make a request to the universe, make sure that you understand your request fully. Are you emotionally neutral or filled with joy when you make your request? Many times you can make a request with anger or frustration as the underlying feeling. This makes your request impure because there are issues within it that restrict your intuition from bringing you your desire.

By looking at your request more deeply, releasing any negativity you discover surrounding it, and loving yourself more, you can make your request with neutrality and love. So,

- Meditate before you make your request.

- Ask your higher self, in your dream state or in self-hypnosis, to reflect on your question to see if it says what you want it to mean.

- Journal your request.

- Take a walk to become clear on the issues behind your request.

- Sit with yourself and be honest in your investigation. If you are unsettled, ask yourself why you are so frustrated and angry around this situation.

- Become as clear as possible about this request and then make it in a calm and loving state of mind.

Requests that are steeped in anger go up the tube bouncing side to side like a bright red, zigzagging rubber ball. The response then includes the frustration in which the question was originally formed. This helps you realize how truly angry you were. The universe is simply bouncing back to you, with intensification, what you already felt. This is the way you can recognize your mental and emotional state of affairs.

The universe is letting you know it is time to go inward, reflect, and make peace with yourself. So why not put out a request for assistance to heal your wounds? Why not ask your higher self to participate in that healing? Those requests to the universe will be returned with love when you send them with love for yourself, along with the recognition that healing is necessary and possible.

When you are focused and aware, you can easily learn from your experiences and make different requests.

Question: We often tell our clients to make somewhat open-ended requests by saying, "I would like this, God, or something better." Is this useful?

You are wise to say, "This, God, or something better," because you are unable to comprehend the scope of possibilities that might meet your desires. You may say, "I need a new car," and a new car comes to you with a large monthly payment. If, instead, you say, "I would like proper transportation so that I may move around with ease and joy," then the universe can bring you what you think you desire, which is a car, or something better—because you have expanded your request. You could receive an almost new car with minimal payments. Or someone could loan you his car to keep it running while he is out of town for the next six months. Then the car is free! Many possible options can appear. By concentrating on the benefits you desire, your request is less restrictive. This allows both the flow of possibilities and the benefits to be greater.

Question: What responds to our requests?
Is it Source or our higher selves?

Your request with your desire floats up the tube of light from you through your higher self to your full self then on to Source. The response comes back to you from Source through your full self to your higher self and then to you. Source is that core energy within the center of All That Is that is held in love.

To create, you must see yourself as God, or creator in your world. However, just as you are God and able to create, there are other gods before you and above you. This is because your world is a conglomeration of worlds, upon worlds, upon worlds.

For example, the cells in your body are a part of your organs, and your organs are a part of your physical system. Your physical system is a part of your energy system, which is functioning in this reality as a part of your higher self and full self. Your full self, which is larger than your higher self, also functions in realities beyond this one. The layers continue.

To simplify, your request flows from a thought or desire up your tube to your higher self, to your full self, which is less connected to this reality, density, or incarnation. The request goes to Source to be fulfilled.

When you request something from Source, there are layers of energies, densities, realities, and beings that could be a part of fulfilling your desires. However, it is more important to focus on clear, neutral, or joyous requests than it is to investigate and know exactly how it all works.

You could see it like going to the grocery store and placing your order for a fully prepared holiday turkey. The grocer says, "We will put you on the list. Your turkey will be ready to be picked up the day before Thanksgiving." You made the request, but you did not think about the birthing of the turkey, the farmer who raised and delivered it, or the cook who prepared your turkey for you. You simply picked it up, paid for it, and gave thanks.

Focusing too much on how the turkey will arrive at the store can actually slow, or even stop, the request from being fulfilled. It is more important to focus on your order so that you receive the right size turkey for your needs. After you receive it and eat it, you can reflect, "Was it a large enough turkey? Does everyone in the family still eat meat?" By considering the answers to these questions, you can change your next year's order to either a larger turkey or a smaller one with the supplement of a tofu turkey. When you are focused and aware, you can easily learn from your experiences and choose to make different requests next time.

Why not have a safe, easy, and enjoyable life?

CHAPTER 11

Blocks to Intuition

When you block yourself from seeing the truth,
you cannot accurately interpret the
activities around you.

Question: What blocks our intuition?

Intuition is your access to Source and All That Is. You could see your intuition like a funnel cloud that descends into your world from Source. It brings with it a cloud of information that you translate into meaning for yourself. You could see it either as a friend who is kind or an energy tornado that moves through your world with reckless abandon.

As a spark of light from Source, you have the desire to expand. This is your nature. When your expansion is blocked, your intuition (in the form of higher self wisdom) eventually steps in to bring about movement.

When you fear and ignore your intuition, it can sneak up on you and cause destruction in your life, forcing you to look inward and grow. By "destruction" we mean that it carries away your current beliefs and moves them around in such a way that you cannot place them back into your existing belief system without thoroughly reexamining each one of them. That would be the restructuring of your world, the rebuilding of your inner home after a tornado has passed through it.

If your blocked intuition escapes and moves through your world in such a rampant and destructive manner, you know that you have not accessed its wisdom for some time. In other words, it is like the pent up energy in an active fire hose that is turned on but not yet flowing. The pressure is such that your intuition must release. When it opens up, it swings about like a wild fire hose that no one is holding. This is your higher self's wisdom coming forward in destructive ways. We say "destructive" because when you hold strong beliefs and judge things as either right or wrong, you build a defensive structure around yourself that must come down to allow for growth, clearer vision, and the ability to understand intuition.

In other words, let's say you have a vegetable garden that you tend and adore. An army comes toward your garden to demand that you give them all of your produce. If you were an intuitive person, would you not want to receive a warning of this ahead of time? Would it not be of benefit to you to see them in the distance coming toward you? In that way you could take from the ground those vegetables and seeds you deem to be essential, place them in your backpack, and leave your garden before they arrive. You could go to the mountains and wait there for the army to move through the village. If they only cause destruction by pulling up all of your vegetables, that would be fine because there would be no harm to your person. This is listening to your intuition rather than to your old beliefs and judgments.

You may say, "Oh, but they will harm my garden. I must stay to defend it. I believe that would be the right thing to do."

And we say to you, "Make decisions wisely. As a farmer alone in your garden, is it a good idea to defend yourself against an oncoming army that desires to control your area whether or not you like it?"

We suggest that it is best to take a stance of nonresistance and move temporarily to the mountains. This allows you to have all the food you will need, for you have placed that in your pack. It allows you to have a good view of your world, for you can see far and wide from that higher perspective. And you can know when it is safe for you to return to your land and bring your seeds to plant again. It is your intuition at work when you move beyond your wall of old beliefs and allow yourself to see clearly.

It is time to break out of old beliefs and judgments and be more accepting of your world.

Question: Are you saying that our beliefs can block our intuition?

We are simply letting you know that when you block yourself from seeing the truth, you cannot accurately interpret the activities around you. The tornado runs through your life when you don't allow yourself to move out of the box of beliefs and judgments you have created for yourself. When you live in a box, it is like living in a 1950s-style house in which everything has its place. You don't talk to certain people. You don't consider or think about anything outside of your box. You go off to war seeing the world through your own version of a 1950s' lens.

This causes destruction for you because your belief system is stuck within a particular box of rights and wrongs. You are bound within the confines of your own beliefs. This is a way of being that is unproductive for you. Eventually, it causes you to crumble from within. Your system was not meant to close down in such a way that it disallows intuition. You were meant to expand and grow.

These beliefs, or boxes, might have been imprinted or, perhaps, created by your analytical mind in an attempt to make you feel safe. When you have lived in boxes for so long, one day your intuition, that part of you that is wise, bursts forward to wreak havoc on your overly organized world. It teaches you to look outside of your box.

Question: What beliefs do we need to change in order to be more intuitive?

We recommend that it is time to break out of old beliefs and judgments and be more accepting of your world. By doing so, your experiences become easier for you. The tornado that brings forth wisdom becomes a friend instead of being a destructive force that must knock you down.

Your intuition tornado is there for you as your access to Source. It is a funnel of energy that brings your intuitive wisdom to you through the ethers. This tornado can come in many forms. If your anger and small-mindedness have fed the ethers, then the clouds may be angry. The wind may whip up and your world could be in peril. By "world" we mean your old limited thinking, your negativity, your approach to life. If, on the other hand, you have appreciated your world—the clouds and the wind—and have seen all things as good the way they are while knowing that you can make choices and changes, then the funnel cloud of intuition and wisdom becomes your friend. It may elevate you and allow you to see things from a new perspective.

There is no destruction unless you require it to bring you the light you so desire. If you have closed down your access to the light, which is your memory of who you truly are, then the funnel cloud must burst open your roof to awaken you. If your box has been closed down for a long time, the wind can be destructive and the light can be piercing.

But if you desire to become open to your intuition, you will see the funnel cloud coming from a distance, and you will love and appreciate it for what it is. It then loses its velocity because its point has been made. It has asked you to pay attention, to listen to your inner world, to love yourself and those around you. By your doing so, when it arrives at your door it is your friend. It is calm because it has been understood.

If there are those around you who still need destruction in their world in order to awaken to their higher truths, then the funnel cloud will go knocking on their doors. It leaves your door alone. You achieved the enlightenment that was meant for you to achieve with greater ease.

Question: Can there be group awakenings of our intuition?

Yes. There are events such as these group awakenings every day. The reason your news broadcasts appeal so much to you is that many of you desire to learn through another's experience or growth. This is useful. In other words, you witness destruction in another's world through war, weather, or accidents. You say to yourself, "Oh, that could have happened to me!" Then you go into your heart. You find love for yourself and appreciation for your world and those in it. By doing so, you allow the destruction to move on to another who has not yet awakened.

When many see disastrous events on television where mass destruction is experienced, their hearts open up as a group. This destruction causes them to awaken. It moves around the pieces in all of their lives and causes the spectators to reconsider their own basic structures. It causes the need for a rebuilding. With rebuilding, people consider the design of their world and how they might see it differently in order to be in more alignment with their higher selves and with Source.

Those who build blockades and require that the old beliefs be adhered to will find it hard to move ahead.

Question: Do we need to experience destruction to awaken our intuition?

Remember, there are those who experience the storm physically and those who step aside physically yet involve themselves at an emotional level. The tornado moves through their emotional world.

There are also those who no longer need to experience destruction at a physical or emotional level. They can be neutral and receive the information most gently from their perch on the hill. The compassion they feel can be paramount in their own awakening. By allowing things to be the way they are, they are not engaging with the destruction. And by not engaging, they have more time for themselves. They can love themselves more. They can appreciate their world, love it more, and by so doing, they have the capacity to bring more light into their experience.

Often, when you are personally involved in the physical and emotional destruction and reconfiguration of your system, you have no time to love yourself more. You are bound by the responses you make to your world. We are simply suggesting that by using your intuition, by accepting who you are, by stepping out of the need for physical and emotional destruction, by allowing your neighbors to have their own experiences, by letting down your walls of beliefs so that you may see, you become more neutral and allow yourself to be more intuitive.

When you are neutral, as in the garden and army example, you can see the army coming in the distance. You can pluck up the vegetables that are right for you at that time. You can choose to place them in your pack in a timely manner. You can walk away from your garden, and the army does not seek you out because they have not seen you. You have not become a focus in their world.

If, on the other hand, you stay and fight with the army and tell them, "This is my property. Get off!" they will laugh. It is wiser to listen to your inner wisdom, take your pack of seeds and vegetables, move to the mountains for a time, and enjoy it there. You are not a coward. You are a wise one who has listened to your intuition and expanded your perspective enough to leave the physical and emotional drama behind. You have embraced your intuition.

Allow it to be your time of connection with the light, your time to remember who you truly are. You are simply in another location when you move to the mountains. You can enjoy this new location for its differences and uniqueness, and you can truly leave your garden behind for a time.

Question: You keep using the attacking army analogy. Are you letting us know that something like this is coming?

No, not necessarily. However, your world is in turmoil at this time. There are factions that have been let loose which are looking for destruction, looking to overtake the easy prey in your world. If you prepare to move through this with nonresistance and the use of your intuition, you are fine. Those who build blockades and require that the old beliefs be adhered to will find it hard to move ahead. Their worlds will experience destruction. Whether it is physical or emotional will depend upon the need of that individual at that particular time.

At some time, all individuals are required to awaken to the light and the love through accepting themselves. When you deny your true reality, when you accept only those thoughts that have been passed down to you, you limit yourself. As expanding beings, limits are destructive. They do not allow for growth. Therefore, these limits must burst open when you expand. You may see these bursts as destructive, yet they are required for you to move ahead. They are a part of who you are as a connected, intuitive being. You must expand, grow, and live in the light with love to survive.

Question: Is destruction to awaken our intuition only occurring on this planet, or is it also occurring in other parts of our galaxy?

The universe expands and contracts in creative ways to allow for or force the growth of the individual. The word "individual" can be defined in many ways. You could say that a galaxy is an individual. You could say that a planet is an individual. You could say that a human is an individual. A cell is an individual. There are no limits to defining an individual. It can be defined as large or small. Therefore, these laws of the universe apply in your world. Speaking about areas beyond your world is inapplicable at this time. Focusing elsewhere is beyond you, beyond the scope of your world. It is unfulfilling and, therefore, inappropriate.

If the mind becomes trapped into seeing narrowly and concerns itself with that which is beyond you rather than you, then your world implodes because your concept of yourself is incorrect. Your world must include you. You must be a part of it, within it and accepting of it. The microcosm and the macrocosm are reflected in each other.

Question: Is there anything else that we should discuss right now?

Your attention to yourself is paramount. Find ways to love yourself more by appreciating yourself in both small and big ways. You will then make progress in your world. This appreciation allows for your intuition. The more you appreciate anything, the more your intuition is there for you as your friend.

Remember that a funnel cloud of intuition can be like a friend in your world. Everything can be your friend when you love yourself more because everything is within and without you. There is no difference between the inside and the outside. Loving a particular funnel cloud allows you to appreciate any funnel cloud within your world, within your being, and within your body. By loving your funnel cloud rather than fearing the changes it might bring to you, you can be alerted at all levels when it is important to know "what is."

Question: Can there be energy blocks that prevent intuition?

Yes. There are blocks of every kind that you have devised in your world to keep yourselves safe and separate from potential growth and change. These blocks have not worked successfully and cannot be successful because they defy the laws of the universe. Wherever you have blocks—wherever you have allowed yourself to be blind—you will experience destruction of some kind. And by "destruction" we mean the overpowering of negative or narrow beliefs that keep you from receiving your intuitions. This is the destruction of old worlds and old ways of being to allow for your expansion into a new way of being and seeing.

CHAPTER 12

How to Keep Your Intuition Flowing

*Negative beliefs of fear, judgment,
and competition boomerang back to you.*

Question: *How do you clean out your tube and keep it clean for your intuition to flow?*

Your tube of light is the device that connects you to Source and allows you to function in this reality with the emanation of a body. This tube, or beam, of light that brings to you intuition and life force energy, allows you access to who you are. It also allows you to remember who you have been and determine who you would like to be. It is your access to the wisdom of All That Is and all that you are.

To receive intuitions more easily:

- First, feel the desire to have a clean tube of light.

- Second, ask that it be cleaned. Your higher self can clean your tube on a regular basis, but you must ask that it be done.

- Third, ask to become aware of any remaining blockages in your tube. When you ask to see, you are granted sight, either immediately or soon thereafter.

- Fourth, choose to take action to clean your tube of the remaining blockages. Choose to do all that is in your power

to heal past wounds, misunderstandings, and mistakes
so you can receive your lessons through the light.

Once clean, you must have the further desire to keep your tube clean. This continues the process. If you were to pretend that maintenance is not important, then the likelihood is that you would defer maintenance again and again. If you choose to avoid maintenance, you are choosing to ignore your tube. It will then become less functional or useful. Ignoring something is as much a choice as doing something. You may prefer to think that things should be done for you automatically, but they are not. You must determine and identify your desires and proceed from there.

Also, if you have a thought or feeling that needs to be resolved, it will reoccur until you consciously choose to make a change in that area. Choosing is a form of completion. Choose to take action.

Your beliefs determine the results that you allow yourself to receive in a timely manner. Depending on your belief system, the cleaning of your tube can occur in a variety of ways. If you desire, you can ask to see all of your blockages and have your tube cleaned immediately. The difficulty is that your belief about timing and possibilities may not allow this to occur. In such a situation, the benefits would not be forthcoming. This is why we suggest that you might begin by asking for those things you believe you can receive. Why not ask for something simple so you can feel good about creating the results?

Finally, commit to work with the light in the future. Make an agreement to see, listen, feel, and respond. Keep that line of communication clean so you can know when you are on target and when you are not. You are requesting to be part of the team that cleans and maintains your tube of light. This choice connects you to the Source of All That Is, allowing you to participate in the creation of your world while being more fully conscious.

You participate in the creation of your world, whether you know it or like it. You can fully create those things you desire or you can just partially create them out of a lack of love or light. In this system, you can create more with more love, which can result in more light.

When you ask to experience expansion and growth on a regular basis, you participate with Source in bringing about those experiences that will expand you.

Question: What can we do to clean out old beliefs?

Your belief system holds you within your world. These beliefs are of your own choosing. They set the vibration for your experience. If you desire to have beliefs that allow you to expand and grow, then you must truly desire to acquire those different beliefs. You may say to yourself,

I desire beliefs that allow me to expand and grow.
I release old beliefs, unkind thoughts, and negative activities
that have limited me in the past.
I take action to achieve this now.

Negative beliefs of fear, judgment, and competition will boomerang back to you. Soon you are living in a limited world rather than living in the limitless expanse of who you truly are. By choosing to release old beliefs, you are halfway there. Then, take action. Whenever you find yourself limiting yourself with the thought of, "I can't do that," catch yourself and think, "Yes, I can. How may I go about that?" Let your creative mind, your intuition, your access to Source, activate your field with ideas of new possibilities. Let yourself enjoy these new thoughts. Let them filter into your being so you can feel them mentally, emotionally, and physically.

While you practice letting go of old beliefs and practice changing, keep this exercise of activation to yourself. Your experiences must be fostered and nurtured in order to grow. If you share these ideas before they are integrated into your vibrational system, others who are not as adept at accessing Source will most likely criticize your will to change. They will tell you that you are unrealistic in your expectations and that you should set your sights lower.

There is no reality that is "realistic" other than the one that you determine to be so for yourself. What is realistic to you may not be realistic to another. If others have not yet accessed Source and all the possibilities therein, reality will be more limited to them.

When you ask to experience expansion and growth on a regular basis, you participate with Source in bringing about those experiences that will expand you. This is the feedback loop. You ask, receive, respond, receive, respond and receive. The stream of information flows continuously.

Question: What else can we do to bring in more light and intuition? Sometimes it is really difficult to initiate change.

When you love yourself more and intensely ask Source to, once again, bring in more light, you send forth a great desire to halt yourself in your tracks and turn your train around. Your higher self and full self join you in this intense desire. Your full being calls back the light. When the light feels your intense desire, it responds and returns, allowing you to change.

This is why some Christians interpret this action as being "born again." The light descends and life returns. You are born again of the light. It is an experience that everyone can have.

Prayer is a powerful tool you can use to bring in more light. It is necessary at times when you have fallen into darkness. One negative thought after another can cause the light to retract to some degree. That path can take you into a downward spiral from which it is difficult to return.

When you pray, which is simply making your request with significant intensity, you gain the attention of those energies that are available to support you. You could see these energies as angels or guides in your realm. Your love for yourself alerts them to come forward and assist you in bringing the light forward.

These angels and guides are available to assist you at all times, but your desire to function alone, separate from Source, will keep them from you. Instead, you can choose to affiliate yourself with those beings who have your best interests at heart. These angels and guides are available as mentors or coworkers on your team.

CHAPTER 13

Intuition Exercises

*Old thoughts can pollute your space and cloud your
energy field, making it difficult to think new thoughts.*

**Question: In our previous conversations you talked
about the importance of keeping the tube of light clean.
Will using the meditation tools that we teach our clients
and students—such as grounding, bringing in the light,
setting an energy boundary bubble, and circulating
energy—also be useful in developing intuition?**

Any process that strengthens your access to Source, and thereby your
intuition, is paramount. And whatever you can do to increase the light
that emanates from your human system, the more intuitive, or truly
functional, you will become.

The first step is to have great love and appreciation for you. Desire
the light to be within you. Upon your request, the light of intuition and
life force energy descends down your tube into your body, or physical
universe. Your body is your creation, or habitat, while you are experiencing planet Earth. Everything in existence has its own experiential
universe, and your personal universe is held within that larger universe
of planet Earth.

As you bring in your light from Source to fuel this experience, you
create an energy field by emanating this light from your body. This
energy field, or aura, can extend outward from your body up to a couple
of miles, depending on how much you desire to create. Let's say that it

expands outwards as far as you can see if you are creating a great deal or only a few inches outside of your body if you are creating minimally.

Set an Energy Boundary Bubble

Your area for creating is generally within your realm of sight. You can bring your energy bubble in around you to arm's length for manageability purposes. Remember, this area can vary in size depending on your desires. If you were to consider this energy space around you as your energy bubble, you would want to keep it clean and clear of any refuse or pollution. You would then be able to see your intuition clearly, breathe, and create well within it. By maintaining your energy bubble, you can create a defined space for yourself where outside influences are deflected and creating is easier. This is the goal for maintaining your space.

Cleanse with Light

As the light comes in from Source to the top of your head, fills your body, and fills your auric field, there is a washing away of old thought forms, or emissions, that you created over time in your everyday thinking process. This cleansing of your space allows you to think clearly about what you desire.

When you are bringing in more light and your energy is cleansed, moving, and grounded, you are better able to access your intuition to create consciously.

Old thoughts can pollute your space and cloud your energy field, making it difficult to think new thoughts. This is why it is difficult for an old dog to learn new tricks. Habits of thinking remain in your field unless you choose to release them. Remember, everything requires choice. The older you become, the more thoughts you have had and the more polluted your energy system can become if you have not kept your energy field clean.

Cleansing takes place when you desire to bring in the light and then bring it in through the top of your head. It also takes place when you exercise, for this, too, activates your energy. Exercise releases toxins, not only from your physical body, but from your aura as well. Movement should be encouraged at all levels. The purpose for movement is to allow for growth and change.

You can do breathing exercises to keep your lungs moving. You can do eye exercises to allow your eyeballs to feel more flexible in their space. This opens the pathways to seeing things in new ways. You can hang upside down in a contraption or hang off of the edge of a bed. This allows the blood to rush into your head for a while, rather than away from it. Jumping up and down on a trampoline starts the energy to move as well.

Dancing is high quality movement, as long as it is pleasurable for you and not intended purely for the enjoyment of another. Swimming and running are also high quality movements as long as they are not overly taxing on your system. Playing chess and reading are both excellent because they move your mental muscles and challenge your way of thinking.

These exercises move the energy in your system so you can move out old habits of thought and ways of being. The light cannot enter if you are immobilized by old ways of being. There must be available space within your system for the light to come in. Increasing the light within your system is necessary to initiate change.

So why not create a regular cleansing system for yourself?

- Upon awakening, choose to move your body.

- Choose to activate the energy field that surrounds your physical being.

- Also, make an effort to find thoughts of love for yourself.

Amazing things can be accomplished by the use of a grounding cord.

Ground to the Earth

When you arrive in this existence called planet Earth, you connect to the system of thought that is established here. One of your attachments to this experience is your grounding cord from the base of your spine to the center of the earth. It keeps you anchored to the earth. You can also use your grounding cord for cleansing by dumping old energy, thoughts, emotions, experiences, and ways of being down it. Just visualize all these things going down your cord to the center of the earth to be recycled. You can also imagine grounding cords coming out of the soles of your feet and descending into the earth.

Most people do not realize that all of these amazing things can be accomplished by the use of a grounding cord that is attached to the base of the spine. If you view the average person's grounding cord, you will see what appears to be dirt that has accumulated over the years. This is because you must make the decision to keep your cord clean. To avoid that problem, first request that your grounding cord be constantly cleansed with the light. The light can remove and dissolve old thoughts and refuse. Second, request that your grounding cord always be filled with light for a continuous flow of energy.

Circulate Your Energy

Meditation of any kind is useful for quieting the mind, allowing you to think more clearly. The meditation technique of circulating, or running, energy moves the life force energy down through your body, past your chakras, and out your grounding cord. Like taking a shower, it cleans your energy and invigorates your system.

Keeping that path clean will increase your access to intuition at every level of body and mind. This technique for energy movement and management releases old thoughts and energies, making space for new creations. It intentionally moves the light of intuition and life force energy throughout your system. This activates your system more fully and assists you in becoming aware of the possibilities for creating.

Most people assume that their body is a given. They received it at birth and whatever happens to it after that is out of their control. We suggest that nothing is out of your creative control. You are a creator being and have options with the treatment of your body at every turn. You can create a better platform from which to create by consciously choosing to love yourself more, access the light, and move life force energy throughout your system to activate your cells.

When you are bringing in more light and your energy is cleansed, moving, and grounded, you are better able to access your intuition to create consciously. Because of that, we recommend the systems of energy movement and management we have discussed. We highly recommend any activity that involves your full being of body, mind, and spirit so that you may create from every part of you.

Question: Beyond these meditation techniques of energy movement, how does hypnotherapy fit into this discussion of intuition?

When you use either self-hypnosis or hypnotherapy, you are activating the creative part of your mind and accessing wisdom so you may create what you desire. With these two techniques, you can create systems of thought or activate thoughts that cleanse your system so you can create anew. For example, you can create self-hypnosis audios to cleanse your system, bring in the light, and start moving your energy.

Beyond this, hypnotherapy can be used for viewing "what is." By going into your inner world, your unconscious, you can see your current situation, grasp its meaning, and choose to accept your current pathway or decide to create a new endeavor. It gives you the opportunity to become aware of what you have created, make a decision about it, and decide what you would like to change or create next.

We highly recommend hypnotherapy as a tool for creating. Instead of watching a television show about someone else's life, you can focus on your own inner television to watch your own life's progress. You can then determine with greater confidence how you would like to proceed.

Question: I believe that we can use hypnotherapy to go inside and alter our beliefs. Is that true?

True. When you enter your unconscious, the imagery that unfolds gives you a succinct understanding of where you are now. These images allow for self-reflection. You can examine the current belief system that holds your current experience in place. If you find a belief that brings about an activity that is no longer pleasing for you, you can choose either to alter or release it. Through accessing your unconscious, or creative mind, you can accept new beliefs about yourself that can completely change your experience of reality.

Hypnotherapy can truly help you move ahead when it is facilitated in a shamanic or personally involving and empowering way. This creative, transpersonal process is different from hypnotic programming that you might experience in some therapies, on a stage, or in advertisements. Programming by another entity involves becoming more unconscious rather than more aware of the situation. Remember, you are meant to be aware and make choices for yourself.

By actively accessing the unconscious mind in hypnotherapy, you can see your current situation correctly and in the current moment. You can choose to alter images to alter the results. This is the creative process. It is very different from allowing another to program you. At this time in your evolution, the goal is to allow for free thinking and awakening on your part. You have come forward and requested this grand opportunity.

CHAPTER 14

Trusting Your Intuition

*You have options to connect or disconnect in
every moment of your being. Every small act
is truly grand in its consequences.*

Question: How can you trust your intuition?

Your intuition is what connects you to Source. When you are fully connected, you are whole and pure. You may trust that equation. When you lack sufficient connection to Source, you become distrustful of yourself.

When you are connected and know it, you trust your intuition. You know you are God in your universe, and the information that you bring in from Source simply "is" for you. Because you are connected to it and you know it, there is no doubt, no questioning.

When people distrust their intuition, they simply need to go back to the drawing board to discover where any possible disconnection to Source may have occurred. Did you disconnect through a thought, a feeling, or an incident? Trace that energy back to that experience and relive it to discover where in that activity you let go of your connection to Source. Then reconnect through determination and healing. If you are still unsuccessful, you can return to one of the techniques we have discussed.

For example, if you stub your toe and blame yourself for having done that, then you have not only injured your body, you have also injured your mind. You have compromised your trust and have disconnected from Source. As a whole being, it is inappropriate to hate yourself, and blaming yourself for having stubbed your toe is a form of hatred. This hatred causes a disconnection. It introduces negativity into your space. This removes you from your experience of being God. You are putting yourself down, loving yourself less, feeling inadequate, and feeling unworthy of the light. This small act of stubbing your toe can sever the ties you have with Source enough to interrupt your ability to access intuition.

You may say, "Oh, but it is such a small act. How could that disconnect me from Source?"

And we say to you, "You have options to connect or disconnect in every moment of your being. Every small act is truly grand in its consequences." All acts either maintain your connection with the light or interrupt it. Unknowingly, you ask the light to halt its connection with you when you consider yourself to be less than whole. The idea of being less than whole, less connected to Source, brings about that reality of separation.

Blaming and hating yourself is the beginning of your downward spiral into darkness. You lose yourself and blame others. Because you are lacking in yourself, you feel that you must take something from others to be whole again. But if you can notice your every small act, correct yourself as quickly as possible, and reconnect yourself to the light, you will be fine. Your intuition will flow again and all will be provided for you.

The only time you injure yourself is when there is a lack of love or focused light within an area of your body. Love and light go together.

This is your homework: Catch yourself every time you put yourself down, judge another, or criticize anything in your realm. We are not saying that you should go brain-dead and assert that everything is fine. We are saying that you disrupt the flow of energy into your system when you criticize anyone or anything in your realm. Be discerning rather than critical.

When you notice something, it simply is. You are neutral about it. You notice you stubbed your toe. You say, "Oh, I stubbed my toe. I'll love it now, hold it in my hands, and let it feel the warmth I have for it. I'll stroke it and tell it I'm sorry that I ran into the doorjamb. I'll appreciate it. I'll apologize to it and let it know I will be more attentive and alert in the future."

By doing this, you bring your toe back into your reality. You encompass it with love. You fill it with light. You acknowledge the realm in which you create, and you set the energy boundary around you to include your toe. You bring conscious awareness to your space and to your toe.

Your goal is to love yourself, appreciate yourself, find joy in your experiences, and let the light flow freely through you.

Acknowledge that you had forgotten your toe's presence when you stubbed it in the past. You had ignored it. It was not part of your whole. Had it been included in the love and appreciation you have for yourself, it would not have bumped into that doorjamb, for when you love and appreciate something, it is included in your reality. It does not need to gain your attention through injury. The only time you injure yourself is when there is a lack of love or focused light within an area of your body. Love and light go together. When there is less love, the light cannot descend. When there is less light, the love retracts, for there is less need for its attention.

By fully appreciating your toe and bringing it back into your circle or realm of creating, you bring love and light to that area. You encircle your toe and return yourself to wholeness. In wholeness you are connected to your intuition, which is your access to the information from Source. When you are whole and connected, you can trust your intuition.

Your goal is to love yourself, appreciate yourself, find joy in your experiences, and let the light flow freely through you. Wherever you find a space that has less love or light in your mind, body, or experience, purposefully bring both love and light to that area.

Question: What techniques can you use to access and trust your intuition more?

There are many techniques you can use to help you connect with your intuition, including meditation, dream work, and hypnosis. You can use self-hypnosis to look into your unconscious to discover what obstructions might be lurking there that keep you from connecting with your intuition and achieving your desires. The technique of hypnotherapy can take you deeper to heal those wounds and bring you back to wholeness.

There are other techniques that are useful for clearing your energy space, such as grounding, bringing in light, and circulating or running energy. However, no technique works if you spend your day feeling and saying that you cannot trust your intuition. These cause both your tube of light and the intuitive information within it to retract because you have told them you do not trust them. This demonstrates a lack of love for yourself and your natural processes.

The light will also remove itself from that location of thought and you will have less and less trust in your intuition. It will be a downward spiral. Again, it is up to you to choose to do those things that allow you to trust who you are. Truly, it is a bigger picture than saying you do not trust your intuition. It is you not trusting your full self.

Question: It seems difficult to receive information when there are so many electronics and outward influences bombarding us. Others, including unseen energies, also want to influence us in our decisions. How can we break through all of that to become more independent and intuitive?

Again, you must ask to create through your own being in your own realm. This desire creates the space to bring in intuition through the light. By asking to be connected, you are. Remember, seeing yourself as a victim actually creates just such a scenario in your world. You will become subservient if you see yourself as a victim of electronics, other people, or unseen energies.

Remember, you are God in your own realm. You create those things that you desire. When you have loved yourself more, you can ask for more. When you are ready, you ask to receive more.

If you can love yourself enough to see yourself as able to function in a world that has electronics and individuals who want to influence you, you can take all of this lightly and laugh it off. You can say to yourself, "I am God in my realm. I connect to Source. I bring in my light, which is all I need to survive in my realm. This connection brings me all the intuition and life force energy I need. The light flows through me and gives me the reality I desire. If I desire to be foiled and brought down by the negativity around me, I can easily do that, too. That can be an experience I have. However, I choose to connect to Source at this time, and I do so. I walk freely in a world that is often negative and can bring many people down, for that is their desire. I let them be in their world. I choose to walk in the light."

You can see yourself as living in an energy bubble of your own creation, unaffected by negativity. Things that are undesirable to you bounce off your boundary bubble. If negative energy—which is energy lacking light—flows in your direction, you see it being redirected to the outside of your bubble where it does not affect you. You are safe and secure inside your world. Your world is all that matters. The outside world, as you define it, is immaterial to you.

Create the rules for yourself. Realize that the main rule is to connect to Source, and make that your priority.

Question: How do you elevate your vibration to be unaffected by negativity?

You take yourself to a place of higher vibration by asking to be there. Request to be filled with love so you may receive more light as you quietly walk with humble joy and grace among other people. See yourself as being extracted from the world of negativity. Imagine yourself levitating quietly from darkness into light. See yourself walking one story above the crowd. Feel yourself free of negativity as you walk in the light. You can then elevate yourself to a higher vibration. It is through your desire and your request to be unaffected by negativity that you arrive at this new higher place of existence. It is that simple.

Question: If it is that simple, why haven't many of us been able to do that?

You have listened to and believed in the information from others more than you have listened to and believed in yourself. You have subjugated yourself to the realm of other beings. You have not acknowledged that you are whole.

Create the rules for yourself. Realize that the main rule is to connect to Source and make that your priority. Do not listen to television, radio, or any other propaganda media that try to convince you that it is wrong to think for yourself. Do not let the media tell you that you must rejoin the group of the walking dead. Extract your mind from negativity and welcome the light.

Question: *So how do you function successfully in the everyday world while trying to stay away from negativity? How do you go to the store or hire someone to work for you while avoiding that interference?*

By taking a stance of nonresistance, or neutrality. You are acting as though there must be a pushing away of all those who are negative. Instead, remain in your well-defined space of light, your energy bubble, and keep that energy clean around you. Eliminate any leakage of light from your space into another's space. Let others be themselves. Let go of the idea that you must convince others to change. Keep your light around yourself. By doing this, you can go wherever you like and be with whomever you wish while achieving whatever you like on your chosen path.

Question: *How do you make sure that you are making the right request of your intuition?*

To receive meaningful information from your intuition, you must first specify your desire so the universe can understand your request. What do you want? Here is an exercise that will help you clarify your desires:

Sit quietly until you feel the love for yourself bubble up within you. Then, get up, walk around, and feel yourself being present in your body.

Now, sit down, feel present, and let the love bubble up some more. Specify your desire by asking yourself, "What experience do I want to receive?" Imagine yourself in that experience. Feel yourself receiving your desire.

Can you receive it now or do you need to alter something?

Alter the image until it feels right. View it from every perspective. Turn it around so you can see it from every direction. Check again to see if it still feels right.

If you locate a belief that blocks you from receiving your desire, acknowledge it and congratulate yourself for finding it. Choose to engage in an activity, such as self-hypnosis, hypnotherapy, dream work, or journaling to dislodge that old belief. Replace it with an appropriate understanding.

Know that you have everything you need within you to accomplish your goals.

This exercise may require a few repetitions. Once you have clarified your desire, take a moment to view your image from every possible angle to see if there is anything else you would like to alter. If there is, make that alteration. Repeat this until you are sure your intended creation is right for you. You may want to engage in contemplation, journaling, or hypnotherapy to dislodge old beliefs and make the space for receiving your desire.

It is like baking a cake. You want to mix in the right ingredients before you place the pan in the oven. It is your concoction, your creation. Once it is baked, it is yours to consume and to experience.

Again, it is up to you to choose to do those things that allow you to trust who you are.

CHAPTER 15

The Qualities and Abilities of an Intuitive Person

To be an intuitive person, ask to be well connected to Source, practice being well connected to Source, and apply what you learn. Then all the qualities of an intuitive person will be yours.

Question: What are the qualities of an intuitive person?

As an intuitive person, you remember that you are God. When you bring forward the memory that you are creator in your realm, you feel good about yourself. You laugh a lot. You remember that not only are you God, but so is everyone else. You respect others and the boundaries you and others create. You appreciate the uniqueness that you bring to your life. You appreciate everyone for their uniqueness. You feel confident and free to create. The idea of victimhood or someone controlling you has no place in your world.

Imagine that you see the plans for creating your world on a table in front of you. You focus on these plans and go about your creating. When you come to a challenge, you think quietly and carefully, ask for professional advice from your intuition through your higher self, and listen to the answers while remaining neutral and in charge. This is a joint venture between you and Source.

You assimilate information by doing such things as napping, meditating, walking, and letting yourself receive answers that are right for you. You think well of yourself and appreciate who you are in every aspect. This love of self gives you the platform upon which to stand and create.

You do not fear others. You do not fear lack in your life. You let go of any negative thoughts around the possibility that you might not be supported with an answer. You look at situations from a creative point of view, knowing that the answers will come. You assume that you have everything you need to create in your realm. You focus on the goodness that dwells within you and allow that to propel you ahead.

You believe in yourself. You enjoy creating. You enjoy the people around you. You see them as good within their beings. Some may have ignored or misused their energy and are, therefore, less able to access Source for themselves. That is all right. Briefly notice this fact and know that at their core level, they have all they need to survive and grow. Let them address their own shortcomings so they may overcome them. Let them create for themselves. You can brainstorm with them to help them remember they are God, but your focus must be on your own experience and not on changing the experiences of others.

As an intuitive person, you honor the creative aspirations and processes of others. You see that each individual has his or her own path. You inspire by example and appreciate them with joy in your heart. In this way you support their development and growth rather than interfere with it. You smile knowing that everyone evolves eventually.

Because you have requested it over and over again, the ability to have greater awareness is granted to you.

Being intuitive involves accessing your information and then applying it. You know that follow-through is important. For example, if you request to know how you can lose weight and the universe shows you an image of working out at a gym, you quickly locate gyms in your area and choose one. You then go to that gym and participate in the activity you saw in your mind's eye.

When you put into practice the information that is brought to you through your connection to Source, you honor it. You appreciate yourself and keep your connection strong by taking action and following through. Your intuition then continues to bring you the information that you desire.

When you neglect to apply the intuitive communication you receive, the tube of light responds by retracting slightly. The more you neglect the information, the more the tube retracts. When the tube retracts, the information becomes fuzzy or foggy because the light that comes through the tube is not completely connected to you. Your world begins to crumble from the inside out. You begin to question your intuitions at such a time. This is the way intuitive people can become less intuitive. They ignore the messages, so the messages come less frequently.

To be an intuitive person, ask to be well connected to Source, practice being well connected to Source, and apply what you learn. Then all the qualities of an intuitive person will be yours.

Question: What abilities are associated with the use of intuition?

When you are well connected to your tube of light, which flows with intuition, your ability to see your world is clearly increased. You have a broader perspective when you connect to your intuition. You can know whatever you desire to know.

You trust yourself because you know that you are connected to Source.

In most situations, you, the intuitive person, have more abilities than others to make sense of the world around you. For example, if there is a challenging situation, you have the ability to sit quietly with that situation and view the different possible outcomes. As an intuitive, you know how important it is to be quiet in your mind, neutral in your emotions, and still in your physical body to receive the answers you seek. You can then translate the information appropriately.

Because you have requested it over and over again, the ability to have greater awareness is granted to you. You can see options in front of you more clearly because the tube of light above your head is well connected to Source and it is clean. The particles of light holding your questions can ascend up the tube, be well received, and descend with the answers you desire.

The everyday person would see you, the intuitive person, as one who can remain calm and make good decisions in the face of a storm. Life appears to be easier for the intuitive because there is less drama, fear, and panic. You trust yourself because you know that you are connected to Source. You know the answers will be forthcoming. The answers come because you have a relationship with the light that you have nurtured over time.

The information you bring through your intuition will depend upon your areas of expertise and interest. It will also depend upon how cleaned out and well maintained your tubes have been over many lifetimes. Exceptional abilities are available to you once your intuition is securely attached to you and you have developed a great working relationship.

If you focus upon staying quiet, neutral, and still you can request and receive an answer that is applicable in your world. It is best to focus on your own world before you move on to general information about others or the world at large. However, the ability to see, know, and experience all things the universe has to offer is an intuitive ability that is available to you in time.

Question: Can intuitive people talk telepathically to animals or people on the other side?

Surely. Being telepathic, speaking with animals, communicating with those who have passed, and understanding your world are all abilities of an intuitive person. You are meant to use your abilities.

When your tube of light, which flows with intuition, has not been used for some time, your ability to be telepathic is, of course, diminished. So it is best to focus on increasing your abilities to make good decisions in your personal world. Then you can progress to a world of greater telepathy.

You smile knowing that everyone evolves eventually.

CHAPTER 16

Making Better Decisions Using Intuition

Review your question. Ask it. Wait. Listen.

Question: How can you make better decisions using your intuition?

Ask to make better decisions by using your intuition. Make this your focus. Believe that you can do this. Trust that it is within you to do this. Take action to move ahead.

For example, sit quietly, let your body become still, and meditate to calm your mind. Ask that your emotions be quieted as well. It may take a while to become neutral if a situation is bothering you. You may add exercise into this formula to help you focus more clearly on who you are in the present moment. Also, through exhausting yourself physically, you can burn off mental chatter and emotional garbage that may have held you down. All of these activities can give you better access to Source and, thereby, to your intuition.

As you sit quietly, loving yourself, believe that you have the ability to access Source. Trust that all information will come forward as needed. Review your question. Ask it. Wait. Listen. Stay in meditation for a time to ensure that you have opened the intuitive channel to Source. Notice if there are any energies interfering with your reception. If so, ask that they be cleaned out. Check the connection from the top of your head to Source to see if the light is flowing freely. If there is difficulty there, ask that the situation be improved.

In other words, as the creator in your world, take action by maintaining your body, which allows you to be here. Sit with joy in your heart and feel truly grateful for who you are. Know that the answer is forthcoming.

---

*Take on activities with joy in your heart
and trust in your mind.*

An answer may come to you in meditation or it may come a little later through synchronicities or creative ideas. Beware of the trap of telling yourself, "Darn it. I didn't receive my answer. Something must be wrong." Saying these things puts you in a downward spiral of fear and doubt, and it blocks your intuition. Let go of the activity of self-judgment and remind yourself that you are God, the creator in your world. You have the ability to access Source; all answers are waiting there for you. It is simply a matter of dedication and time.

After your appointed amount of time in meditation, let yourself get up and go about your day knowing that the answers are forthcoming. Take on activities with joy in your heart and trust in your mind. Let other people be themselves. If they are negative in their worlds, let them be that. Focus on yourself with joy. In this way, the intuition has time to travel down your tube, or column, of light and arrive in your conscious awareness. Perhaps you will receive your intuition in another meditation when you are quiet. You can also receive it when you are exercising and being more present in your world. You can receive it when you are laughing and having fun, for these are good ways to clear your intuition channels. You can also receive your intuition in your dreams and through noticing synchronicities.

Focus on all the wonderful ways the universe can bring information forward. Let your focus be gentle to allow the universe to bring information to you in ways that may also be unfamiliar. This is quite different from holding on to your familiar methods of reception with intensity and tenacity. This can squeeze—even close—your tube. Preconceived notions, beliefs, and judgments can also block intuitive information from coming through.

When you receive your information, give thanks. Then, when you are ready to do so, you can continue the conversation by asking more questions on the same topic or you can ask questions on another topic. This continuing process keeps your system well oiled and on a continuous path of progress.

Living a life filled with intuition is a worthwhile experience. It is why you are here.

Question: What can interfere with making better decisions with intuition?

You cannot make better decisions with intuition if you turn the process into a job. When the job becomes unpleasant, intuition has no interest in coming forward. If you love yourself and enjoy the experience of being you, the light particles that hold the information you desire will come forward and answer your questions. In this way you are participating fully in your life. That is you being whole.

When you are depressed or upset with your circumstances, the light retracts. It becomes dim, making it harder for you to see. It is like a gray day when it is difficult to see the horizon. Yet, you can see quite clearly when the sun peeks out.

To make better decisions using your intuition, you must believe that the sun can shine and you can request its presence in your world. This belief allows you to trust yourself. In that trusting state, you feel joy, accomplishment, and a healthy sense of pride in the fact that you are God in your realm. This is a positive stance. The joy you feel allows you to ask a question purely and be open to the response.

Putting pressure on your intuition is exactly the opposite of what you should do. This act is born in fear and creates more fear. Instead, appreciate yourself for making good decisions. This is why vacations can be useful. They allow you to feel better about yourself. Any break you take to appreciate nature or your body is good for you. It acknowledges that you are here in a physical reality by choice, and you believe that it was a good choice.

A life with less love, light, and intuition is filled with fear and gray days that take you in a downward spiral. In contrast, living a life filled with intuition is a worthwhile experience. It is why you are here. You are here to experience yourself as creator in your realm, nothing less. Until you accomplish this, you keep coming back to the same, or similar, experiences. It is your goal to move ahead and expand. With love for yourself, look up and see that the light is waiting there for you. Simply bring in the light, which is supported by your love.

PART THREE

The Path Continues through Other Dimensions

CHAPTER 17

Why Intuition Is So
Important Today

Freedom occurs when you love yourself more
and there is more light within you.

Question: In other channelings, Anne has intuitively seen where areas of existence are eventually pulled back into Source. Could you please explain this vision?

Imagine yourself as a grand creator who expands into the universe to have experiences as the light. When you are complete with your experiences, you call back your light to your nucleus to contemplate expanding again. This is the natural evolution that everyone experiences. In the microcosm, you are birthed and then you die. This is the same as the light expanding outward and then retracting. Eventually, you retract from every experience you have and you return to the nucleus, or Source, of who you are.

No matter what you are experiencing, you eventually return to the nucleus. It is similar to breathing in and breathing out or to the ebb and flow of the tides. You can have an experience you are enjoying or not enjoying, and you will still be returned to Source at some time.

The way you spend your life's experience is up to you. Your choices are nonending. If you experience yourself in misery because you blame yourself or others for your predicament, you will have regrets when Source retracts and pulls you back. You will regret not having been the grand creator you had hoped to be. This judgment is a lack of wholeness. So it is with this lack that you return to wholeness. Eventually everything, which has not returned to wholeness on its own, returns to wholeness to be expanded outward once again. It is up to you how you experience your world.

Question: Today it feels important for people to learn more about intuition. Could you speak to our sense of urgency?

The clouds are rolling in. If you assume that tomorrow would be a better day to learn intuition techniques, then tomorrow it could rain. It is best to work when the sun is out and the conditions are correct for the support you need to go within.

Some may say, "I will be saved when I change dimensions." And we say to you, "Save yourself now." Make yourself more fluid in your thinking. Allow yourself to love yourself more today so that you may have new experiences. Become more intuitive. If you wait for this so-called "dimensional shift" you hear so much about, you will make it your god, and it is not good to make anything your god. You are your own god, creator in your world.

Question: Some people believe that we will be moving into the fourth or fifth dimension as a planet. Is that what is happening today?

No, not exactly. Your spirit is moving ahead. Your body is busy catching up. Things are shifting at different levels, at different times. It is not as though the dimensions are shifting at the same time, in the same way.

It is as if you were using Lego blocks to build a dimensional wall. Because you are in the process of building, the wall is continuously uneven until you are complete. Once complete, however, your wall has the power to levitate magically off the planet while you are standing firmly on top of it. As you lift off, you have the experience of becoming lighter, and that is enlightening. This new dimension is exciting and free of the physical world. You experience the physical world at a subtler level; you experience yourself as free and more able to move about. This freedom occurs when you love yourself more and there is more light within you.

Question: Anne has had the vision of people partying in a house. A few leave the house to take positions in the yard on individual hexagonal pieces that fit together and activate when enough people stand on them. As the house starts to burn down with the partiers in it, the hexagonal floor lifts off carrying all the people who had chosen to leave the party and stand on it. Is this image similar to that of the levitating wall above? Is this our future?

True, very much so. You have an enlightening experience in which you relieve yourself of the past and are present in your world. By being present and loving yourself more, you allow yourself to lift off. You allow yourself to leave behind all those who were caught up in the external world of temptation. You let go of the material world. That subtler energy, or light, that fills you is a different vibrational experience than you are mainly having today. It is one that allows you to appreciate yourself more, for you are less critical, less dense, less judgmental, and less wrapped in the drama of your world than you were before.

This is the direction in which you are headed. By "you" we mean those of you who desire to leave the density of judgmental thinking and manipulation, which you have endured for so long, and move ahead in the light. Those who choose to remain in the density and drama will do so. Remember, everything is by choice.

You have access to all dimensions at all times, but your density and beliefs keep you primarily in one or another.

119

Question: Will both groups you just mentioned remain on the Earth? Will some lift off to other dimensions and others stay in the density of this experience? How does this work?

The desire to be anywhere is up to you. The dimensions shift and change regularly depending on your desire for an experience. You could have a third-dimensional experience in one moment and a fourth-dimensional experience in the next. You shift through dimensions quite regularly without knowing it. You could have your emotions existing on one level and your mind on another. Again, it is more fluid than you think.

When we say, "existing in a certain dimension," it only means that more of your energy is on one level than on another. You have access to all dimensions at all times, but your density and beliefs keep you primarily in one or another. When your vibration changes by loving yourself more or less, you go up or down the dimensional scale. You become heavier with judgment and lighter with love. When you become lighter, you see more and your experiences change. You are more able to create and you create more quickly.

Question: The image where we stand on the hexagonal pieces in the yard makes it seem as though we are changing dimensions. Is that true?

If you desire, aspects of you can have access to all dimensions at all times. It is like playing the scales on the piano. You can move up and down. But you have little ability to move when you are dense and lethargic. The likelihood is that your movement will be limited unless you experience freeing, loving thoughts. When you have freeing, loving thoughts, you can move to a higher dimension. But the likelihood is that you will move back down unless you are comfortable at that new level of freedom.

Your vibration is the element that allows you to shift. When your vibration becomes faster, the particles move more freely and quickly. This gives you flight. It allows you to transport yourself dimensionally.

You could see it as first vibrating slowly and then speeding up so the particles become excited and move around. As they move, the opportunity for movement is increased, allowing you to fly to other worlds or other dimensional experiences with only a thought.

You could see dimensions like horizontal bands that cross you, a vertical being encompassed in a vertical tube of light. The light at the bottom of the tube is more solidly yellow. As you move up the tube, the light becomes lighter and brighter until you can barely see it at all. This change in the light structure allows for movement between dimensions. This is a continuum. The device, the vertical tube, exists on all dimensional levels. It is simply a matter of where the majority of your energy resides. This will determine the dimension you believe you are experiencing.

This freedom of movement between the so-called horizontal dimensions allows you to come and go into different realities. All of these realities are still in your world. You still reside within your own column of light, but your experiences can change.

Question: Is it like being in a room where many dimensions are occurring at the same time and other beings are there but we just cannot see them?

Yes. Many things occur at many levels at the same time. For example, in your dream state your energy is subtler and your reality can shift and change more easily.

CHAPTER 18

Orbs and Other Dimensions

*You engage these orbs and respond to them.
In this way, some orbs are like couriers
from other dimensions.*

**Question: What are orbs, or spheres of light? We are seeing
more of them all the time in our photos. Are they from
another dimension?**

Orbs are evidence of dimensional shifts in your reality. They let you
know that you can have experiences with other dimensions. They allow
you to notice that everyone and everything has freedom of movement.

Often, orbs are thoughts of beings that come to you from afar. They
are curious about your world. For them, it is like going to the zoo. They
can drop into your world and see what you are doing.

If you choose, you, too, can be an orb. You can send your consciousness elsewhere to see what is occurring there. This form of movement is
available to you at this time. It gives you the ability to commune with
nature.

*You may communicate with anyone or anything
at any time whenever you desire to do so, as long
as your beliefs allow you that opportunity.*

Some of these orbs are here to experience your world. Others are here to be of service by planting thoughts in your mind that otherwise would not have occurred to you. They do this by gaining close proximity to you and letting you think their thoughts. It is similar to standing next to a friend who suddenly says, "Let's go to this great restaurant named Jack's," and you say, "I was just thinking of that!"

Information is transferred from one person or orb to another by being in close proximity through physical location or mental connection—or, more succinctly, through the connection of spirit. When an orb is in your proximity and it desires to communicate with you, and when you are open to communicating with it as well, then communication can flow freely. By being "open to communicate," we mean that you must have enough open space between the light particles in your mind to accept the communication.

You may communicate with anyone or anything at any time whenever you desire to do so, as long as your beliefs allow you that opportunity. This opens up your world of possibilities. When you are communicating with orbs, you have many more friends. But some orbs are wiser and more light-filled than others. So just as you desire to be with physical friends who are of like mind and positive, you can feel the same desire with your orb friends.

Question: You said that orbs are thoughts, but then you said they are beings. Could you clarify?

Some are thought forms. If you look carefully, they have very little movement to them. They are bouncing around with little life. These are emanations, or refuse, that are released from the mind. They bounce around like plastic bottles on the ocean. They are orphans. They are belief patterns that float in the ethers. They can gain strength by floating into and unintentionally merging with each other.

You could say that beliefs or thoughts float in the ethers without any real energy to them, but they still have a life of their own. If you look, you will notice that these patterns of energy, these orbs, hover above churches and lecture halls where everyone is thinking the same thoughts. This is why it is good to clean out old thinking from an environment so that everyone can think new thoughts.

There are some other orbs that are pieces of energy that were left behind when someone died and otherwise transferred to another dimensional reality. These are parts of a person that have been left behind either out of neglect or purposefully for the intention of communicating.

There are also some orbs that have more energy, more movement, and more possibilities than others. These are more like energy devices or probes for communication with you. They are extensions of larger realities that enter your reality to communicate. You engage these orbs and respond to them. In this way, some orbs are like couriers from other dimensions. There are so many options and experiences to be had with orbs.

You are an energy pattern that distributes yourself to have experiences. You can send part of yourself, in the form of an orb, to experience another reality.

Question: You had mentioned that orbs are like probes. Are we humans like probes for Source to give Source an experience?

Yes. You are emanations from Source. You are experiences to be had. At the core, there is no difference between you and an orb, even though you would like to think so. But there are differences between you and orbs on many levels. That is another discussion.

Question: Are some orbs beings like us?

Very much so. You are an energy pattern that distributes yourself to have experiences. You can send a part of yourself, in the form of an orb, to experience another reality. This is when your primary experiences are in one location, or dimension, and another part of you exists in another dimension, or vibrational experience. You gain information and bring it back to yourself. It is another situation similar to dreaming. You go off and have an experience while your body lies quietly at home.

Question: Do orbs have intuition?

No, not exactly. They are intuition. They are communication. They are that connection to Source. They are that distribution of energy from Source that actively seeks out experiences in your world. We are not speaking here of thought form orbs that float around. We are speaking of the orbs that are more filled with the light and have chosen to take a journey to communicate with you. They are dimensionally related to you through thought. They generate movement through desire and intention to be in your proximity.

If you were to see your world as filled with bubbles of light with which you can communicate, you would enjoy your experience more. This would open up a world of possibilities for learning and growth. Air may look empty to your naked physical eyes, but it is not. Everything is held in love and filled with light.

If you were to understand your individual world as a cup of love that holds the light, and within that cup are thousands of possibilities for experience, then you would be filled with joy and greater expectations. You would see your world filled with so many options, choices and experiences. Instead of looking at the space around you as empty, bland, lonely, and separate from God, you would see yourself as filled with God. As God, every possibility you could imagine is within your world, within yourself.

CHAPTER 19

Animals and Ascended Masters

*Everything is connected to Source
and has the ability to be aware.*

Question: What about animals?

Animals are supported by love and filled with light, as are you. Their options abound. They have choices. They have creativity. They experience their world just as you experience your own. You and the animals experience each other and, as part of the whole, you both can communicate as well. You overlap when you experience each other, so you can co-create.

Animals are the same as orbs. You can experience orbs, and orbs can experience you. You can experience animals, and animals can experience you.

Question: Does a tree or a rock communicate with Source and have this same light?

They do. They access Source and receive information. All things are connected. Therefore, everything within you is within everything in existence. Nothing is left out of the loop, so all things are both created and creators. A rock is a universe unto itself. It experiences its world and creates from within it. It is different from you, but it is of wholeness and, therefore, is a creator in its realm.

Your experience of the tree and the rock are within your realm. They descend to you in the light. The more you love them, the more you love yourself. The more you treat them with respect, the more you appreciate yourself. This is why it is important to embrace your world fully and treat it with love. That is the macrocosm that allows you, as the microcosm, to love yourself more.

This is why people who desire to save the planet are often loving beings. However, when people judge others for destroying the planet, they block their light with their beliefs and negativity. Every activity has the potential for being an expansive experience or a negative and darkening one that can limit one's life.

When you access Source, you access wisdom and endless possibilities.

Question: Is there anything else that comes in the light besides intuition and life force energy?

Light is the full accessing of Source for everything you need. There are other beings that also come forward in the light to be with you. You can invite them in. You could see it as a freeway tunnel that allows all invited guests desiring to communicate with you to descend and all requests you have to ascend. When you access Source, you access wisdom and endless possibilities. You access the endless relationships you have with yourself and with others.

Remember, as a whole being, you are one. As an individual experience of light, or spark, you are many. Therefore, you can call upon the other aspects of you to experience yourself in community. This would be you experiencing others as friends. They can be animals, people, or other beings. Whatever you desire to have in your world funnels down that column of light from Source into your being. This is how you create your world.

Question: Are people who have died working to develop their intuition also?

It is specific to each individual. Some choose to grow and some choose not to for a time. Each person is a world unto him or herself. The differences abound. It is like asking if someone who dropped out of school, became a drug addict, and lived on the streets in misery was having the same life experiences as a monk who spent his whole life meditating on a mountaintop in Tibet.

Everyone desires to move ahead, and some are more aware of this desire than are others. Some who have died no longer contemplate this world and are free to move about. Others are trapped in the same old thinking, so they bump into you at times believing that you are in their world. That is another discussion.

Question: What about ascended masters?

As you become wiser and more adept at bringing in the light of intuition, the wiser aspect of you, which you call your higher self, merges more fully with you, and you walk in the physical world with more light. You are, therefore, more of a light being. This is why some people say that Jesus, and others, emanated so much light. They were fully accessing Source more often than the typical person. Their tube of light, which included intuition and life force energy, was more fully descended into their individual worlds.

People say that these beings are "ascended beings," and we say that it is all in the way you look at the process and describe it. You could say that they are higher, brighter, and subtler in their vibration. And if you were to see the light coming down and filling their physical universes, you would also say that their higher selves were becoming more fully incarnated and present in their physical universes. Therefore, while in the physical, they would have greater access to more information in the light more of the time. Remember, it is your aim to do this too.

As you bring more light into yourself and your world, you create instantaneously with only a thought. Once you do this, you are complete in this realm and can move on to other experiences in other realms. You may choose to expand elsewhere into more subtle realms where the light within those experiences is subtler. In those realms, there is less physical mass.

Question: What about other dimensions and ascended masters?

You experience levels of existence as being either dense or subtle. The term "dimensions" is simply used to describe the variety of experiences you have, from the most dense to the more subtle realms. As your personal vibration increases in velocity, you are able to move through dimensions at faster speeds. If your mind is filled with belief patterns that do not allow for travel through different realms of existence, you remain in the dimension that is most comfortable for you. The heavier the thoughts are in a particular dimension, the denser is the reality because heavier thoughts will weigh you down.

This is why you must release old patterns of thinking in order to ascend and why you say ascended masters look so light and bright. They have let go of the density of thinking and the attachment to matter. They have allowed themselves to fly, or speed up their reality. The vibration within their reality and within themselves has sped up, which gives them the freedom of movement through dimensions. Therefore, they can have experiences of themselves in different realms of existence. This expanded experience is entertaining to them.

If your mind is filled with belief patterns that do not allow for travel through different realms of existence, you remain in the dimension that is most comfortable for you.

CHAPTER 20

Friends in Other Dimensions

You are a part of the whole of existence.

Question: How does the energy of an era in history or the energy of a particular environment play into our intuition?

It does not, any more than any energy plays into your reality, unless you desire it to do so. You can accept or reject anything. If you desire the era and environment to support you in growing and moving ahead, then the opportunities will avail themselves. You can bring forward these supportive energies for your world whether or not they are coming forward for others. Your reality is your own, and you can always choose to activate your space to experience personal and planetary growth through the greater use of your intuition.

However, the overall opportunity to access your intuition and wisdom through the light can be more available to you in certain eras. The energy pattern that is descending into your realm at this time does include more particles of light than it did in 1980, and particularly more than it did in the 1950s. If you choose to access these light particles and participate with them in your creating, you have the opportunity to co-create more than you had previously. You can choose to clean out and participate with joy in preparation for the increased energy available today.

At this time in history you can see more energy patterns of light dangling around you, ready to play. These are information patterns that you can access for greater understanding. If you look closely at your light, you will also see that there are many particles you may consider to be friends from other realms. Not only is your tube of light accessing that which you have seen to be your light, but it is also accessing that which is you from other realms, which you see as friends.

Through holding the desire to be whole, pure, loving, and accepting of yourself, you make choices that are good for you.

The realm in which you currently exist in waking reality is one world of experience, but there are many worlds beyond that. You are God in all of your realms of existence, although you may notice that you generally focus in one realm more than others. Your focus can shift from one reality to the next. Your focus for creating can change as well.

When you dream, you participate in activities that are different from those in your waking realm. You dream as creator in another realm of existence. This lets you know that your energy pattern is available to you in more than one realm at a time.

Look closely at your aura, or light pattern, that is emanating from you at this time. There is the request there to invite a multitude of friends from other realms of existence to play and create with you on your playground. Playing with energies from other levels, dimensions, or realms of experience gives you access to more information, more of the time, because you are blending your dimensional experiences. These new experiences can be most enjoyable and entertaining.

As you clean your tube of light and release the fear of seeing what is, your sight will be improved.

Question: Are these friends different parts of ourselves, beings visiting us, or ones we visit outside of this realm?

Remember, you are a part of the whole of existence. Therefore, all things in your reality are a part of you. However, in this separate experience you call Earth, you have separated out energy patterns that differ between entities to identify yourself as one and others as separate identities. From the image of separateness these emanations of light are your friends. Your higher self allowed them into your experience because these interactions assist you in changing and growing.

You may have noticed these friends as orbs in photographs. You may have experienced them as guides or loved ones in your dream states. In times of need, you may have felt them around you reminding you that you are loved. At times they may have cared more about you than you cared about yourself. And now that you are requesting that more light be brought in so you can be more present, you can notice this support.

You may experience orbs, beings, or emanations of light around you when you are having thoughts of camaraderie or fun. Simply ask to see them more clearly. As you clean your tube of light and release the fear of seeing what is, your sight will be improved.

At this time, you are co-creators in many endeavors, or games. You are not dependent on one another, nor are you better than one another. You are simply enjoying the company of those you find to be interesting.

How you experience this activity of co-creation in the light is up to you. If you deem it as bad or wrong, it will dissipate. If you choose to live more in your heart with the light flowing through you, that will become your reality. These choices are important. As an expanding being with well-flowing intuition, you can create and co-create quickly. When your energy is stuck, you will change less. It is your choice to play in the light or return to the darker experience.

This choice is available to you for you have chosen to bring in the light to see more clearly with your increased intuition. Those individuals who are unable to see clearly because they deny this continuously available choice may think you are a bit crazy for seeing things they cannot see.

Through holding the desire to be whole, pure, loving, and accepting of yourself, you make choices that are good for you. You hold the premise that you are supported by love and connected to the light. This is your protection as you move ahead.

CHAPTER 21

The Factors of Creation

For every world there is a creator, upon creator, upon creator, and the realms of existence are multiple. In this discussion we are focusing upon your realm, in which you are God, or creator.

Question: Could you describe the creation of our world some more?

Your world is a microcosm of a larger world. In your world, you maintain a system that you call your body. It has within it many organs and processes that require love and attention in order to maintain its functionality as a physical body. Your body is a conglomeration of many systems, or universes, within your world. Look within your physical body and realize that you are universes upon universes. You are a well maintained system within yourself. This is no different from the galaxies around you. If you were to realize that you are in charge of your body and your world, you would be impressed with yourself and love yourself more.

For every world there is a creator, upon creator, upon creator, and the realms of existence are multiple. In this discussion we are focusing upon your realm, in which you are God, or creator, for that is what matters to you. Once you develop yourself fully and access your intuition to survive well and create the things you desire, you can move ahead to experience other realities beyond this one. That is another discussion.

Question: Could you explain further how life force energy, intuition, and the tube of light work together?

To explain further, your life force energy comes with your intuition through the tube, beam, or column of light that is your connection to the Source of All That Is. There is no actual physical form to the tube. This tube allows you to create. Whenever you have a question or a desire for creating, you send that question or desire up the tube and the answer comes back to you with intuition and life force energy. This brings about creation in your world. There is nothing magical or mysterious about this process. It is the way in which things work in your world.

In the beginning, you, as a spark of light, desire to have an experience. You find yourself drawn to this particular reality, this life, because it seems interesting to you. You descend through the light as a stream of life force energy and intuition into this reality and give birth to your world. You ignite your experience of being whole, creator in your realm.

A tube of light specific to your experience has a pattern within it designed for you. You could say that the light has life within it that moves through your system and gives life to your world. This tube is the device that continues to maintain the definition of who you are. It reminds you that you are whole, yet separate, in your world. It helps you identify that which is your creation and that which is not.

Intuition is your lifeline of information. It is the device that is personalized to you when you have found a place in the fabric of love to plant your seed for being. The tube with intuition and life force energy connects your seed, or being, to that portion of Source that is available to connect with your seed.

Question: Could you describe love further?

Love is the fabric, or basis, of your experience. It is the beginning—the void—the velvety material from which all things come. It must have desire to receive the light for the light to be received. If love somewhat questions whether or not it wants to experience a reality, it will most likely allow that reality to occur.

The love that you develop and carry for yourself over lifetimes flows with you in the light to ignite the spark that is you. The love, which the fabric of love in the universe holds for you, is held in an energy pattern that allows you to bring forth life force energy and intuition in the light to greet your spark. Love allows for any idea to be planted within its dirt. Love simply is. It is allowing. It is receptive. It is open to all the ideas that come through the light. The light is the more active device while the love is the more receptive.

The light looks for areas in the fabric of love to explore and grow. It desires experiences that are fulfilling. Love must first open its doors to receive the light. If love is not complete and does not feel joy, then the door is closed to the light. Joy is a necessary ingredient of love. If joy is diminished in an area, love is diminished as well. That area in the fabric of love is then unable and unwilling to receive the light.

Love must be available to produce a reality, just as the ground must be prepared with mineral rich soil to receive the seed for it to grow. If love is lacking, little light will be brought forward to that location. Once there is the support of love at your location, you can call in the light with life force energy and intuition to descend from Source down the tube of light to spark the seed. The more love you feel for yourself and the more light you allow to come through your tube, the more able you are to blossom and grow. Through the joy that you have for yourself, you bring forward love in your life.

To explain it another way, love is the necessary fabric that supports you in creating your world. Love holds you and allows you to be. If there is not enough love within you, within a place, or within a relationship, then nothing can be created. If you lose love for yourself, the fabric that holds you in this experience becomes thin and has fewer and fewer threads moving through it. If the fabric becomes too thin, you have the possibility of falling through it. If this occurs, you cannot maintain yourself in your world.

Again, there must always be love to receive the light of creation. Once you are in an experience of life, it is up to you to remember the love that you have for yourself and maintain the flow of light in your system. In this way, the joy of being here may be increased and your experience may be maintained.

Forgive yourself for your shortcomings.
Forgive those around you, for they are a part
of your world and your creation.

Question: What are the ways in which we can love ourselves more?

Look yourself over. Find any place in your physical body where it is lacking love and choose to love it. By choosing to love it, you support that part of yourself. You give it attention. You put nutrients back into your soil. You maintain your fabric. Then ask yourself what you would like to experience in your world. Once the idea comes to you, the light descends and the creation is born in your reality. In other words, you love in order to receive, and you create in order to experience. This is the act of being the creator in your realm.

So, put your attention on any area of your body where there is a lack of love and feel more love in your heart for that location. Stay with that location until you can appreciate it. This attention is all that is needed. It is simpler than you think.

For example, you can say to yourself, "Oh, look, there is skin on my knee and muscle and bone are beneath it. I can feel them when I put my fingers there. I am appreciative that blood flows and brings me nourishment throughout my body." Do this with any and all parts of your body. You can do this with your emotional body as well, finding areas that you feel have been wounded or somehow less loved.

Forgive yourself for your shortcomings. Forgive those around you, for they are a part of your world and your creation. Go back to a chosen location in time and space and love yourself more there. Accept who you were in that scenario. Learn from it, relax, let it go, and move on.

It is your responsibility to love yourself so you can create scenarios that you enjoy. The ability to receive and hold a scenario comes first through love. The scenarios then come through the light. When you love yourself more, you can receive a more joyous scenario because the light can come in more fully.

The light can only come in to the degree that there is love. If there is less love in that location, there will be less light. This lack of love and light is the reason you have experiences of physical and emotional wounding. Whenever you are lacking in love or light, the experience will lack joy as well. It will feel like an unfulfilled desire. It is worth going back to the basics to start with love and bring in the light.

Question: If you feel you were at fault in any of your life's experiences, what can you do?

Realize that you loved yourself less at that time. Love must now return to heal the situation. You may say, "Oh, but I loved myself a lot then."

And we say to you, "Look carefully. If you thought you loved yourself a lot, it could be that you were loving your image or your ego." Love cannot seep beneath the surface under those circumstances because you are not fully appreciating yourself. You are only seeing the surface and, therefore, love filters into a false reality that is not fulfilling. To feed you adequately, the love must soak deeply into the soil of who you are. If it only reaches the surface, the nutrients cannot benefit the soil. You must truly appreciate all that you are for the love to soak in.

Question: Are you saying that we must simply love ourselves and bring in light to be great creators?

Yes. It is all very simple and mechanical at the basic levels. Your intuition is nothing magical. It is simply your connection to Source. You could see Source as the great idea in the sky that allows you to be who you are. It is the initial creating, as far as you know it. There are layers upon layers in your world. We are describing the ones that are applicable to you in your experience of time.

CHAPTER 22

Transforming Lack and Disease

Disease occurs to show you those areas from which you have withdrawn your light. Remember, loving yourself with joy is a prerequisite for bringing in more light.

Question: There are many loving people in the world who also create disease for themselves. How can that be?

They may love themselves in some areas but are lacking love for themselves or others in another area. Your world is really just made up of you. If you are upset with any part of yourself, or with another, there is a lack of love in your system.

Let us say that you were physically or emotionally wounded as a child. You did not want to see it. You did not want to think about it. So you pulled your light out of that location in space and time. When it was devoid of creativity, the love was extracted as well because there was no need for the fabric of love to maintain the light. This is what brings about disease. Disease occurs to show you those areas from which you have withdrawn your light.

You can choose to go back to the location and time of the wounding, see it from the broader perspective of you as the creator in your world, and create an accepting scenario there. In this way you bring life, or light, back to that location, which also requires love to be there to hold the light in place. Love returns to satisfy your desire for creation.

Once this new scenario of joy and excitement replaces the lack of energy and light, healing can occur.

Question: Some people create great relationships for themselves while not creating other things, such as material wealth. How does that happen?

Most people love themselves more in some areas than others, so the soil is nurtured with varying nutrients for those different experiences. For instance, some people carefully nurture their relationships, while they give little time to creating wealth. Therefore, their relationships grow and their wealth diminishes. The area you love is able to receive the ideas you plant there. Your intuition is able to access more light for that area because you pay attention to it, ask your questions about it, and make continuous choices benefiting that area of growth.

In that example, there may be other areas, such as wealth, that are somewhat devoid of light. Love, therefore, has not come to that area to be supportive. Again, from the awareness or position of light, you can call forth the support of love. And from the feeling or position of love, you can request to be flooded with light. As you can see, you can approach this situation from either direction depending upon the area in which you feel lack but desire to have abundance.

Find joy in your heart for yourself no matter what you may think of yourself or what you might appear to be to others. You are worthy of love.

Question: Some people seem to have either more love or more light in their systems. If you have tried to increase the one lacking, but have been unsuccessful, what can you do next?

142

Remember, loving yourself with joy is a prerequisite for bringing in more light. "But," you may say, "some people appear to be quite creative and filled with light, yet they also lack love and compassion and are often cruel."

And we say to you, "Let that go. They will find love eventually." It is their lacking that will awaken them. Their pain from their lack of support for themselves will eventually lead them inward. There they will discover the love that the universe has available for them. But they must ask, and it may take time. It may take eons. The universe's love will be there for them, waiting.

You may say, "How can it be that the love would wait for them? I thought you said that the universe's love retracts when we don't hold love for ourselves."

And we say to you, "Love is very forgiving." When you forget to love yourself or withhold love from both yourself and the universe for a while, love waits for you to return. It takes a long time for the love of the universe to pull itself away from you once it has committed to be there for your experience. The love may be saddened that you did not fill yourself with love, but it will not completely retract until you are finished with a creation. By creation, we mean a grand creation, not a single lifetime. The light can retract in a particular situation or lifetime.

Most people need more love for themselves and they realize it. They feel the pain. They want to fix it and feel better.

May we suggest that you go back to the drawing board to discover where you might be lacking. Are you lacking love for yourself? If so, acknowledge that and discover the area, or areas, in which you are lacking. Find joy in your heart for yourself no matter what you may think of yourself or what you might appear to be to others. You are worthy of love. Pets are useful in this exercise in that they can remind you to open your heart and give love to yourself as you do to them.

Perhaps you are in need of more light, more intuition, more creativity. Maybe you have not fully formed the idea of what you desire. If this is the case, the light is confused. It needs direction. Consider a variety of scenarios that might be appealing to you and, perhaps, make new choices. For when you constantly doubt yourself, when you make and remake decisions, the light waits to come down because it is not sure of your choice and, therefore, does not know where to go. It does not know which area to feed with light.

So go within your heart and appreciate who you are with love. If there is something you lack, fill it with desire. Desire to desire. The idea that you don't need something depletes your world. It pulls your energy down. Choose what you desire. Mean it. Really mean it. Once you have chosen one scenario, eliminate the other scenarios from your mind. Be a river of desire so the light can come down with intensity into the area of your desired creation. Then your desire is fulfilled.

Question: If you feel you are so lacking in light, how do you ask to receive more light?

Remember, you must first have love to receive light. Therefore, you must love yourself first. In loving yourself, you see yourself as whole, as already having that which you request. This creates the necessary space for receiving.

Experience the lack as being transformed into wholeness. Use your imagination to see a column of gold surrounding you. Feel every cell receiving the warm light. Know that all creation supports you in moving ahead. You have the ability to make as many decisions—and new decisions—as you like. You can choose to feel the support of love that wishes you to receive the light.

Let the joy of love bubble up within you, knowing that you are appreciated for who you are. If you have trouble appreciating yourself, start by appreciating another:

- Take hold of a pet and pat it.
- Sit with a potted plant.
- Experience the love of a child.
- Appreciate and respect another's uniqueness.

Before going to bed at night, say an affirmation that lets your unconscious know that you continuously desire to see yourself as whole. You can say,

I am all that I need. I am whole. I am love. I am light.
I am my intuition. I am fine. Amen.

See yourself as whole, as already having that which you request. This creates the necessary space for receiving.

CHAPTER 23

The Mud Pond

Your world is whatever you desire to make it.

Question: What is our purpose for being here on planet Earth?

Your purpose for being here is to have an experience on Earth and unfold as a being. As a spark of light from Source, you are here to experience the endless horizon of the universe from your own unique perspective. Source, seeing through your eyes as well as the eyes of all creation, gains different perspectives. This expands the whole.

Question: So, we decided to come to experience planet Earth? Is that correct?

True, very much so. However, you did more than arrive here. Earth is of your devising as well. You created it for this experience.

Question: Some of us have been working on ourselves for many years. Why has it taken us so long to clean out our tube of light, which carries intuition, when all we had to do was ask?

In the past, your asking was convoluted. You forgot that asking was necessary. Then you thought it was too much trouble. You have desired to survive without learning survival tools. You have wanted it to be easy and, at this point, it is not. You could look at it as though you have been soaking in a mud bath and now you must wash off all the mud. You must find the places where mud sticks to you. It is not like getting out of the salty ocean and rinsing off with fresh water. The process is much more involved than that. You have wanted others to wash the mud off for you. You have wanted things to change overnight. This idea is convoluted. It has taken you eons to become this covered in mud, so it takes a while to clean it off. However, you have done better than you might think. You are moving ahead.

It is your self-blame and self-judgment that hold you back. If you were to love yourself more, things would move ahead more smoothly. But every time you find an area that has mud on it, you tend to blame yourself. This is your downfall; it keeps you stuck in the mud. Every time you beat up on yourself, you climb back into the mud bath and then have to clean off the mud all over again.

If you were to look at the tubes of light of those who have been meditating and choosing to grow, you would notice that they are quite clean. The main issue, then, is loving yourself. A vacation or a walk in the park is good for that. Fun and exercise remind you that you deserve joy in your life. Joy propels you ahead. It is the love of being you that makes life enjoyable and keeps you here in this experience.

The mud pond is any experience you have in which you forget you are God in your realm. It can be in any realm of experience within you.

Question: If we created this world to enjoy our experiences, why did we end up with mud all over us?

Your world is whatever you desire to make it. At times, you get into the mud pond because you are curious about it. You want to know what it is like to be covered with mud. You feel that might be an interesting experience. You think it might be a quality you have not felt before. The mud is not wrong, it simply is. By experiencing it you know that once you get into a mud pond it is hard to wash yourself off. That is all you learned. Maybe next time you will decide that the mud pond is an experience you wish to forgo.

This situation is similar to one in which a child burns his finger on the stove. Until he knew it was hot, he was curious about it. The child was not wrong for being curious. He simply wanted to know more about the stove, just as you were curious about the mud. Well, now you know how sticky the mud is and how hard it is to wash it off. If you feel content being clean, then you are not tempted to jump into the mud pond again.

Question: Is the mud pond a symbol of our Earth experience?

The mud pond is any experience you have in which you forget that you are God in your realm. It can be in any realm of experience within you. You can be stuck in the mud of thought patterns that loop around and you see no way out of them. You can blame and judge another being and not be able to see the light beyond the mud.

By asking your intuition to be there with you—by requesting higher wisdom from your higher self—the answers are there for you. You simply must ask, desire to receive the answers, and clear your mind and body to receive intuition and life force energy through your tube of light. This activates the totality of you with creative ideas.

Question: Why has it taken us so long to get out of the mud?

You have been distracted. You assumed that the mud was real. You forgot that you were the creator in your realm, here for the purpose of having an interesting experience. You cursed the mud for being so sticky and uncomfortable. You cursed the planet for having a mud pond on it. You cursed others for not being able to drag you out of the mud pond when it felt as though you were sinking in quicksand. You became so upset with the mud that you fought it, and the more you fought it, the more entrapped you became.

Upon your initial discovery of the mud pond, you would have been fine had you said to yourself, "Oh, look. I placed my toe in the mud, and it's sticky. It attaches itself to my skin. I think I have experienced enough of the mud, so I'll wash my foot and be done with it." You would have understood the mud and felt satisfied with your experience. But instead, you wanted the extended experience. You dove in face-first with a belly flop and enjoyed the pond for a while, experiencing its gooey consistency.

It was not until your curiosity was satisfied upon making it to the middle of the pond that you realized you were stuck in the mud. Upon noticing that you were stuck, you could have said, "This is hilarious! I am really stuck in the mud now. I may be here for the next million years. Well, I put myself in this mess and I will take myself out of it. What shall I do? I think I will lie on my back and let myself float as best I can to the edge of this mud pond. As I float, I will enjoy the sky and the birds flying by, and all will be well. Eventually, I will make it to the shore, and then I will clean myself off and be on my way."

This is the quick way out of the mud pond.

Instead, you said, "Damn this pond. Damn me for getting into it. Damn everything around me. Somebody get me out of here!" In asking another to rescue you, you gave up your seniority as creator in your realm. You hated, rather than loved, yourself. This forfeited your ability to access your wisdom—your intuition—and to heal yourself through love.

You stayed vertical in the middle of the pond and yelled out to anyone who walked by to save you. You cursed them for throwing you life preservers that were inadequate. The angrier you became, the longer you stayed in the pond. Eventually, no one wanted to talk to you or help you. They deserted you because you were so unkind to yourself and others. You were left alone. This made you madder and madder until, eventually, you saw that you were your only way out. You finally took the advice that your higher self had for you from the start, which was to turn over on your back and float as best you could to the edge.

At this time in your history, many of you are nearing the edge of the pond. And it has been a long float. But if you blame others for its length you will be back in the depths of the mud again. It is best to give thanks for the sun and the sky around you, as well as the birds flying overhead entertaining you, as you float on your back knowing that the edge is at hand. And, yes, it takes a while to wash off the mud. So why not enjoy the process? Love yourself and feel fine knowing that you have come to the correct decision, that of floating on your back.

Question: How can you say that we are close to the edge of the mud pond? Look at all of the hatred and violence in the world.

Look up to the sky, the sun, and the birds. Focus on the beauty of your realm and its support. Those who are at the center of the mud pond are angry. If you get near them, they will lash out at you, grab you, and pull you down in an effort to free themselves. They will think of you as the life raft that was sent to save them, so they will pounce on you and suffocate you in the process.

When you say to them, "Look! I'm floating. Come float with me," they will assume that you intend for them to ride on top of you. This would benefit no one because as you sink, you can no longer carry them. They would have used you up. It would be over for them and for you. In their panic and lack of intuition, they would not care about you.

You have gained wisdom.

It is best to leave them alone. They must come to terms with themselves, as you have done. They must have no one rescue them, lest they continue to forget who they are. They are meant to be creators in their world. This will only happen if they can come to terms with themselves.

In making your way across the pond, you have accepted and loved yourself more. You have accessed your intuition in the light. That is all that is required.

151

As you float closer to the edge of the pond, remember that you are God in your universe. As you hear those in the middle of the pond crying out to you to be saved, remember that they are creators as well. Eventually, they will gain understanding when they go through the same process you have. They will become exhausted from crying for help, blaming others, and pulling others down. If they simply enjoy their floating when they are left alone in the center of the mud pond, they will make choices. When no one comes to their rescue, they will rescue themselves. You each have all you need within you—your intuition— to make your way to the edge of the pond. You are in the process of making your way home.

You have gained wisdom. You now know that sticking your toe into the mud pond is all you need do to experience the mud. You can look fondly at the experiences you had in the mud because they brought you to the realization that you are your best rescuer. Your best tool is accepting, appreciating, and loving yourself, your environment, the mud pond, the sky, the birds, and the sun.

Your attempts to escape the pond were previously foiled by your desire to use someone else to get yourself out of a difficult situation. When you subsequently beat yourself up for attempting this way out, you took yourself back to the middle of the pond. It has now become evident that blaming yourself and attempting to manipulate others are both poor choices. Becoming exhausted allowed you to realize that you must be who you are, the creator in your realm. Remember, when you quieted your mind, the answers from your intuition led you to realize that you should switch from being vertical in the quicksand-like mud to lying horizontally on top of the mud. You then had to be patient as you practiced loving yourself more.

At this time in history, many of you are tired of struggling through situations in which you constantly manipulate one another. You are ready to be co-creators in your world, which means that you participate with others rather than use them. This is a very different approach for many in your world.

You may say, "How do I communicate with others if they are still nasty and manipulative in the middle of the pond? Who can I count on to be my friends?"

And we say to you, "Look around you in the pond. There are many individuals floating on their backs, planning to arrive soon at the edge of the pond. They are successfully caring for themselves. They are enjoying their experiences. They are not blaming the mud. They are no longer blaming themselves that much. They are accepting what is and are dealing with it. These are your friends."

When you arrive at the shore and wash yourself off, these people will share a picnic with you. These people will sit by the pond, exhausted from the experience of getting out of the mud. You will not find them fighting at the edge of the pond. They know better. They do not want to get back in the mud. These are your comrades. These are the ones with whom you share your meals. They will buy your products and services, and you will buy theirs. Together, you can have good lives.

Once you are on shore, consider your situation. Do you want to sell your products and services to the people who remain in the middle of the pond? They may say they want to buy your life preservers, but if you throw them out to these people and pull them to shore, they will resent you. By rescuing them, you will have robbed them of their opportunity to access their own light. In their opinion, you will owe them, so they will not pay you, but will blame you for everything including the existence of the mud pond. They will say things like:

It was your idea, not theirs, to jump into the pond
with your life preserver to save them.
You should have posted a sign on your property warning
of the existence the mud pond ahead.
You should have made public announcements about
this dangerous pond.

No matter what, they will want to punish you, even though it is not your pond.

This is what happens when you help people who truly need to go within to help themselves. They did not float on their backs to arrive at the shore. Instead, you pulled them through the mud with your life preserver. You are the one who used your muscles to bring them to shore. They had no need of the light or information from their intuition because they were dependent upon yours.

Everyone in the mud pond must rescue him or herself.

Remember this as you sit on the shore. If you look out on the pond and see people yelling for help, you will feel the need to jump in and save them. Remind yourself that you made it out by yourself. Contemplate the bigger picture. Perhaps it is time to take your things and the friends you have made on the shore and say good-bye to the pond. You can make the journey over the hill and into the valley to find a location that is beneficial for you. You can find a place where the light shines and the air is pure, a place where you can be comfortable living for a time while you recover from your mud pond experience. It will be another reality.

If you judge yourself harshly for leaving the pond, you will return and be stuck again. Instead, enjoy the sunshine as you walk around in the grass. Self-acceptance is necessary at this time. Let the experience of living away from the mud pond be a good one for you.

Be fine about being out of the pond.
Be fine about being different and being bathed in the light.
Be fine loving yourself and letting yourself laugh.

Let others have their experiences. Simply keep your distance from those stuck in the mud because many of them will hate you if they see you have made it to shore and are enjoying your picnic. Remember, it is their choice to be stuck in the mud. It will be their choice to get out of the mud by realizing that the answers lie within themselves.

Everyone in the mud pond must rescue him or herself. It is that simple. Those of you near or on the shore came to that conclusion for yourselves and have rescued yourselves. Until others understand this, they will blame you and pull you down. This is what people do when the light is retracted and they forget that they are God, creators in their own realms. They forget that they walked into the mud pond, of their own free will, to have the experience. They wanted to know what it was like, and now they know.

You have learned. You are wiser for it. It is time to move on and let others learn for themselves.

Question: Once you remember that you are God, the creator in your realm, what should you do?

You walk in the world of light. This is like walking in the high mountains where the sun shines on you, the skies are blue, and it feels good. It is a simpler, quieter life, for you have learned from your experiences. You have taken yourself out of the mud. That was an exhausting experience. You are now in a different realm in which you experience that you are God. You were God in the mud; you had just forgotten that for a while.

In the land of remembering who you are, things are easier. Everything is provided for you because you provide for yourself. You no longer ask others to rescue you because you know that did not work. You have friends and you support each other through love and light. You are kind and appreciative of all those who surround you, so you laugh together and make plans to be a community. You do not use others. They do not use you. There is mutual respect.

Question: How do angels and guides fit into this? I thought they rescued us?

Do not cry out for the angels to save you, for they will not. They know that you must make your way out of the mud pond on your own and decide that you do not want to go back there again. In their love for you, they stand aside. The angrier you become, the less likely it is that you will be assisted. The more you love yourself and find your own reasons for being, the more the light shines on you as your friend, bringing you answers from your intuition. The support is all around you when you are willing to save yourself.

There has been a misunderstanding and a belief that angels will come to rescue everyone. Instead, you make the decision and take the responsibility to rescue yourself, and then the support appears. When you quiet your mind, relax, and accept yourself and your situation, you are able to receive direction from yourself, your guidance, your intuition. You say, "Let me think. If I lie on my back this way and I move my arms down, I will head towards shore."

Once you love and accept yourself under these circumstances, you ask questions. You say, "Where should I be focused? In which direction should I lay my head in this pond? In what way should I flap my arms in this mud to move ahead? What should I do with my feet? Should I kick a bit or should I just let them be at peace and let my arms do the movement?"

As you ask these questions, the answers appear in your head. This is your intuition speaking. Here are some simple steps. You could say that you are throwing your DART to hit the target of your desire:

1. **D**esire and decide to care for yourself.
2. **A**sk questions and make requests.
3. **R**eceive answers. Be alert, listen, look.
4. **T**ake action.

If you still do not like your situation, ask more questions. This is how you learn. Ask your intuition for direction. What might you need to do? You can also focus on the following:

- Let love flow from you. (Appreciate your lessons with joy.)
- Let love flow into you. (Let the pond support you with love.)
- Trust more. (Be patient with the mud process.)
- Ask more. (Request intuition.)

- Receive more. (Open to your intuition.)
- Act more. (Act on your intuition.)

Love supports you in your decision to accept yourself. Light warms you and keeps you company because you asked to receive it. Your guides and angels, who surround you, respond to your every request when you have cared for yourself.

Make the decision and take the responsibility to rescue yourself, and then the support appears.

Question: How are these four DART steps of desiring, asking, receiving answers, and taking action similar to the ACT and LEAP steps we wrote about in Eureka!?

The main addition here is to recognize that you must first have the desire to fill your being. Halfhearted desires are not well answered because you are still blaming outside influences for your situation. You must not expect someone or something to rescue you. That is why it is so important to look at your situation carefully. Understand where you are. Acknowledge that you have been in the mud pond for a long time. Then, and only then, do you rescue yourself because you see that is your only possible successful option.

Question: So once you realize that you are your own God and you have taken yourself out of the mud pond, where do you go to have another experience?

Your experiences are within you. All realms are within. As you sit beside the pond enjoying your picnic, take the time to contemplate your desires and your situation. Choose where you would like to go and what you would like to create. Next, take action and follow the light of your intuitions, your ideas. It is that simple.

Who knows what might next attract you? You might say, "Look! That mountaintop over there looks so beautiful. I have known mud. Now I think I would like to know snow." You take action. You walk in that direction. When you get to the snow, you put your hands in it and feel its cold grit. You might say, "This is lovely; I enjoy snow. However, I don't think I will walk on it for the next eon because, even though it is interesting and attractive, I don't desire to be in the middle of it. I was in the middle of the mud pond, and that was enough. I don't need to climb Mount Everest. Instead, I will appreciate Everest from this lower vantage point.

Then you might say to yourself, "Look. There are some interesting animals. I think I'll get to know them. Is that a yak?" So you head towards the animals. You sit beside the herder who milks the yaks and you interview her. You discover how curious it is to live with yaks. You consider whether or not you would like to stay there and become a herder or if you would like to move on. Each step of the way is your choice. There is no magic place or pill to help you make the decision.

Some people say, "I want to know what I should do next. Why can't I see the future?"

And we say to you, "Your life is yours for the unfolding." Your choices determine where you go next. Each individual has individual choices. That is the way your lives are arranged.

You are the creator of your world.
What do you desire to experience?

As a group, you can choose to co-create a world that is beneficial for you. You can choose to co-create with your friends on your picnic blanket. Each of you can also go in individual directions. It is simply choice. You can introduce your desire to the group and see how many would like to come with you on your journey. If their desire is similar to yours, you can go together. Each of you continues to ask questions, receive information, and make choices as you go along.

Desire to desire. Ask that you be shown a variety of options. If you desire to be in a group, you will have companions on your journey. If you desire to be left alone, it will be your solo path.

Ask that your journey will be one of joy and anticipation. The idea that your future is predetermined is untrue. It is true that you made some decisions long ago and true that your higher self guidance assisted you. It is also true that your beliefs accentuate the possibilities and probabilities of what lies ahead. But it is still your choice in every moment that makes the difference.

And given your current choices, asking that the future be shown to you is only useful if you want to see the direction in which you are already headed. You can accept, reject, or change your current path. Assuming that there is a predetermined path assumes that you are a victim in your world. It assumes that you have no active part in the production of your play. We suggest that you have access to all parts, and you may keep or destroy your current script.

Here is an exercise.

- You are the creator of your world. What do you desire to experience?

- If you do not know, take a walk and contemplate your options.

- Go to the playground to see how children play. Do you like the way they interact? Would you like their games to be your games or would you like yours to be different?

- Choose.

It is similar to going to a restaurant, sitting down, and looking at the menu. What would you like to eat? It is up to you. The money is in your pocket. You simply have to decide.

***Question: This scenario seems very similar to the "holodeck"
in the television series and movies, Star Trek.
Is that correct?***

True, that is correct. The options are yours. Once you decide, you
can plug into the computer any scenario you would like to experience.
You can interview those who have already used the holodeck about their
experiences with a specific program or scenario. Did they enjoy it or
was it a harrowing experience? You then decide which coordinates you
would like to plug in to create the reality you want.

Hopefully, you remember that you can get out of the game. If not,
and if you have chosen a challenging program or scenario, then things
will begin to crumble around you until it becomes so unpleasant that
you give up fighting your reality and finally remember that you are God
in your holodeck world. You can stop the computer program to collapse
that experience. You can walk out of that hologram and back to your
original world.

***Question: What happens to those who do not want to
get out of the mud pond?***

There are those who enjoy the mud pond. As long as they enjoy it,
they are fine. The difficulty comes when they judge it as bad. The
minute that judgment moves through their reality, they are stuck in
the mud. When you judge something as wrong, you make it your god.
You give it control over you. You allow it to alter your reality and take
away the fun. When you lack fun, there is not enough space between
the atoms to bring in the light. Your thoughts congeal in such a way
that the light has no access. This is why beliefs look dense when they
congeal together. This is the immobility you experience in the mud.
It looks dark and dense and difficult.

If people truly enjoy the mud, then it is simply their realm of
experience. It is their creation, and they remain God. They can stay
there as long as they like and leave whenever they desire to do so.

Those who blame themselves or others remain stuck in the mud until they remember that they are God and that they can choose their reality. This could take eons. They must determine their desires and act on them. If they no longer choose to participate in the realm of creation, that is also their option. If their desire is to have a miserable time, they will do so. It is not wrong.

Question: How does the mud pond experience relate to disease and emotional problems?

In the physical body, the immobility in the mud can be experienced as disease. It is the lack of ease. It is the lack of flow of creation, or light, throughout the body. It is being stuck in the mud in a particular location where the life force energy cannot flow. This is the microcosm.

You can also be stuck in the mud in your emotions, where you cannot see your way out of a situation. For example, you may be in relationships with the same type of a person over and over again. You complain about it. That is you forgetting that you are the creator in your world. That is you forgetting that you desired to experience misery. By remembering that, you can, instead, create joy for yourself.

Question: Could you please summarize the mud pond experience?

You have come into the world of matter to experience yourself as God, creator in your realm. At some point you forgot that this creation was of your own making. It is one thing to be curious, but it is another to be curious and then forget that you can take yourself out of one experience and expand yourself into another. In forgetting, you assumed that the reality you had created was real and, therefore, you had to continue to experience it.

To get out of the mud pond, all you have to do is remember that you are God and choose to take yourself out of the mud. In the beginning, you put your toe into the mud so you could have a brief experience. Then you did a belly flop into the mud pond to fully experience the mud.

You swam into the middle of the mud pond to see what it was like to have the perspective of one who sits in the middle of the mud and can barely move. This was all good. This was you appreciating yourself and enjoying your experience. The difficulty came when you switched from being God, enjoying the middle of the pond, to forgetting that and assuming that another God had to rescue you from your experience. You mistakenly subjugated yourself to another. You gave away your creative abilities to rely upon another.

In the development of who you are, you are both the creator in your realm and the created. But, remember, all those who are created also remain gods within their realms. You have the ability to create and change your reality at will. This must be remembered to continue expanding your experiences. When you forget that you are God in the middle of the mud pond and demand that another rescue you from a difficult situation, you remove yourself from the position of being creator. As creator, you must remember that you are God to continue this experience. Until you remember, you will wait on the sidelines.

All you have to do is ask your higher self for information about how you can move out of the mud pond, and all the information you need will be given to you. As the one in the mud pond, you could yell out to the people on shore and say, "Hey, throw me a life preserver, and then I will get myself out of here on my own." Alternatively, you could say, "Oh, it is a lovely day. I will lie on my back, move my arms and legs, and float myself to the shore."

These acts are taken by you, as God in your realm. You may ask for assistance from another, but you may not use another to get yourself out of a predicament. You must use your own creativity, as God, to create in your realm while allowing others to create in their realms. You must access your intuition and allow life force energy to flow through you. This activates your cells and starts your body moving in alignment with your mind. This must be your creation. You can then be out of the mud pond in an instant.

Asking for assistance is a form of co-creating. Let us say that a stork flies over you in the mud pond. With kindness in your heart, you ask the stork to come down, scoop you up, and take you to shore. Because you are being the creator in your world, the stork is interested in picking up a human from the center of the mud pond and carrying him to shore. You each think this experience could be exciting for both of you.

In the development of who you are, you are both the creator in your realm and the created.

CHAPTER 24

How We Change

*You have the ability to create
however you would like.*

**Question: How can we change our negative outlook and
become more positive?**

As God, creator in your world, you have the ability to make choices.
These choices take you down the path of experience that you desire. If
you desire a different experience, then you must necessarily choose a
different path.

The difficulty comes when you chose a path that leads to a lack of
light. When you participate in activities that diminish the light, you remain God in your realm but you are somewhat separated from your
world. When you are so far along this downward path, it is difficult to
access the light to make a change. Your desire and asking are not strong
enough at this point to achieve the results you desire.

This is where prayer, or intense desiring and asking, comes in to
make the change. This is the only way you can become fully functioning
again, because your own light has so diminished and love has so thinned
that you are about to blink out. You must ask the universe for assistance
through your intuition, or higher self.

When you pray with intensity to be love and receive light, your full
self—that part of you that is whole and not fully incarnated into this
planetary existence—responds through your higher self. It calls in energy
patterns and gets things moving. You could see it like a committee that
comes forward to answer your prayer. You can ask your higher self to be

the discriminating filter that accepts only those energies that are appropriate for you at this time. In this way, the energies that come to assist you are purely meant for you.

Remember, you are not asking for another to rescue you or save you because that would attribute all goodness to another. That would make you feel less functional and less loving toward yourself. Loving yourself is paramount and matters more in the long run than anything else.

You must be love in order for love to appear for you. By praying to love yourself, your ability to be love is increased automatically. You have rescued yourself. This creates the capacity to receive light and sets you up to make further choices that bring in even more light.

We recommend that you pray to your higher self and to Source to bring love and light to you. Pray that you may exist fully and experience the goodness of your world, which includes your ability to create fully.

Your world is meant to be fully functioning with love and light.

Question: Is there a connection between war and the use, or misuse, of intuition?

Disease and destruction occur when you disconnect from your intuition, forget that you are God, and feel that you must manipulate others to experience your world. This is a mistake. It leads to a lack of those two most important factors, love and light.

If you desire to be fully functioning in your world, then love everything back into existence. Remember, you must love yourself first to receive light. Then if you love others, they, too, might remember that they are God. By loving them, you give them the opportunity to remember. You show them the spark of light that is within them. This reminds them that they are God, rather than victims or non-creators in their worlds.

166

The only way you can be a victim is to desire, or choose, to be so. For example, you may say to yourself, "I have the wherewithal to do what I please. I like to look down on others and judge them. I like to feel better than they are. I like to think of myself as superior when I am not."

And we say to you, "You can only stay superior in your delusion for so long. Eventually, that delusion crumbles and others crawl over you saying they are superior to you. This game often continues and eventually leads to war. This is where many people are now involved. The cure for war commences with love."

You have mistaken your world for a place of necessary deception, denial, conflict, and poverty, which it is not meant to be. Your world is meant to be fully functioning with love and light. Any experience of lack begins with loving yourself less.

Know that destruction is a fully functioning part of this existence. It is to be appreciated. You create and destroy your creations in this world, loving both experiences. This form of destruction involves the deliberate choice for change. It is very different from destruction that is the result of lack. Love pulls away from the latter form of destruction, and the light becomes dim within that creation.

Whenever something is left unrevealed, it must be revealed later in some form.

Question: How do we do escape the experience of victimhood when it is so pervasive on this planet?

To escape the confines of this game of victimhood, you must first see yourself for who you truly are. Are you currently playing mainly the role of the victim or the victimizer? In which situations do you play which role? The game always has players on both sides and, quite frequently, you flip back and forth, even though it is not often acknowledged.

To escape this game, you must first acknowledge that you have played it for some time. Notice how familiar it is to you. Grasp your participation. Feel what it is like to be a victim. Ask to see how you might change the roles, or parts, around. Choose to see all that is involved. Decide which parts of the game you like and which parts you do not like. How does it benefit you to continue this game? Take a true measurement and be specific. Let the hidden aspects be revealed to you. When you see more, you can choose your actions with greater consciousness and confidence.

Whenever something is left unrevealed, it must be revealed later in some form. You will need to return to those scenes to clean them up. By asking to see and investigate a situation, you will be able to complete your task more thoroughly. Once you have reviewed the situation, ask yourself where you would like to make changes to become a different person. If you only say, "I just don't want to be the victim anymore," then you have not clearly defined your desired experience. You must ask for what you want. What would be enjoyable for you? See yourself as a participant in the changed situation. Notice the ways in which you must act differently to achieve a different result.

You may say, "This is too much work. Isn't there a magic pill that I can swallow to change my reality?"

And we say to you, "This is the victim mentality that lured you into trouble in the first place. This desire to go to sleep and be irresponsible in your world is like a drug. It allows you to be lazy and live with less light. It feels appealing to have someone or something take care of you."

May we suggest that this is not "you" talking. As an individual of light, as one who creates as God in your realm, you did not initially desire to go to sleep and ignore your own creating. This desire to go to sleep is the result of convoluted thinking. This desire to have another care for you has been developed over time. Ask to wash this out of your system so you may think clearly once again.

You were originally like a spark of light that started creating and doing well. When you began to believe thoughts of negativity, such as, "I can't do this," or, "What if I make a mistake?" or, "I can't care for myself alone," you went into a downward spiral of thoughts that were both untrue and damaging.

You may say, "How could I create such negativity when I am light?"

And we say to you, "In this world of creating, you are discovering that you are God. You are practicing to become a fully successful creator. You have options to grow and change in any way. Therefore, you can always go forward or backward. You can dismantle yourself and then put yourself back together."

You can cry out to the universe, "Something is wrong with my body, which is my vehicle of transportation. You could say that my train no longer travels along its tracks. Help me! What shall I do?"

And we say to you, "We are here to remind you that you are God in your realm. You have the opportunity to take your train apart and put it back together again. You are not a victim, unless you desire to be so. It is time to acknowledge that your train has been taken apart, and you have all the tools necessary to put it back together. We support you in reconfiguring your train."

Every unkind thought you have about yourself or another takes you down the negative path.

Remember, one negative thought leads to another, just as one positive thought leads to another. A negative thought makes your world become darker and darker because the light has been told to stay away. It is like that train rolling down the tracks. It gains momentum. If you choose to turn the train around, you must first bring it to a halt and consider the situation. How would you like to turn the train around? Perhaps it is time to devise a U-turn in the tracks. That is a conscious choice.

You may say, "I did not choose to be in this downward spiral."

And we say to you, "Surely, you did. You had that first thought, which was a negation of God. You chose to think the thought, "I am not enough in some way. I am somehow lacking." This is you stating that you are unworthy of the light. Remember, when you do this, the light retracts. It hears you and responds. It is a responding mechanism. When the light responds and retracts, you are then less able to bring in more light. This creates the downward spiral."

Therefore, we recommend that you turn your train around and keep it rolling in a positive direction. With the support of love, you can bring in more light. Every unkind thought you have about yourself or another takes you down the negative path. It is difficult to turn around from that place of less light, but it is something you can do.

You may say, "How could these negative thoughts have been allowed into my universe?"

And we say to you, "Remember, you are God. You have the ability to create however you would like. Creating negativity is one of the options in your world. Once you grasp the reality that all possibilities are within you, and that you have choices, you can choose a path that is positive."

If you desire a different experience,
then you must necessarily choose a different path.
If you desire to be fully functioning in your world,
then love everything back into existence.

Afterword

*All That Is is that which emanates
from Source and is in all things.*

We would like to thank All That Is for talking with us about intuition. We have truly learned about the workings of the universe through these channelings. We have seen how we have been victims and have learned how we can get out of that exhausting game completely through choice, and do so with love.

All That Is has added value beyond measure to our lives, and we hope that they have given you precious insights to make all of your experiences more profound. It has been our pleasure to act in service to the whole of All That Is. We feel more in flow with the light and love of the universe.

We would also like to thank those who are walking the path of intuition with us. Their energy and support has made writing this book a joyous journey.

You are invited to join us on this path of intuition and in our ever expanding circle of intuitive friends.

We look forward to receiving more information from All That Is!

Appendix

Key Words
and Phrases in This Book

Comment from Anne and Greg: The following channelings from All That Is summarize the key words and phrases you find in the book. We hope that this continued dialogue expands your understanding. Topics are listed alphabetically below.

All That Is

The whole of All That Is is that which emanates from Source and is in all things. All That Is, which communicates with Anne, is a group consciousness of nonphysical energy beings that comes from a place far from our general experience. They say about themselves, "We are you. We are no different. We are All That Is."

Creation

Basically, love had a desire—a thought—to expand or, you could say, have children. It gave birth to the light. This light expanded into the fabric of love, and created for itself a nucleus, which was Source. This nucleus became its universe. Source, too, wanted to have children, so it put out sparks of light. Time passed and the sparks of light waited in the fabric of love, or space, for more light from Source. Light from Source then extended itself more fully into the fabric of love, seeking out those sparks of light. It filled those sparks, which were ready, with more light, igniting them, so those universes could grow and flourish. Each spark of light created a new universe for itself.

Many universes were created through these acts, and each universe is whole and pure, existing unto itself. The light is forever dependent upon love to feed it and to hold it in existence. In other words, you could see love as the mother of light. It loves all things into existence, holds them, and allows them to experience the light of creation. Within each universe there is a creator, and each creator creates. And as that creator creates, more universes are created. The process continues on and on.

A spark of light can develop into a nucleus, or universe, that can be large or small. It can be the creation of galaxies and planets, as well as the experiences on them. Or it can be the creation of an individual's world, such as the one you experience as your own personal world, reality, realm, or universe. These are the macrocosms and the microcosms within your experience.

Full Self, Spirit

Your full self, or spirit, is all of you, your existence. It encompasses your entire being. It includes those aspects of you that are not reachable from the physical realm.

Your full self is your full emanation of spirit that is distinct in the emanation of light. It is the light that is specific to you. It encompasses all of your bodies and your energy. Your higher self, in contrast, is that aspect of your full self, or spirit, with which you can communicate from your physical form. (See also Spark of Light.)

God in Your Realm, God

You could say that you are God in your realm, your universe, your world, your reality. And within you are other gods, as well, at each level of existence. Each level within you experiences itself as creator. The stream of experience is nonending.

The love that is held for you in the fabric of love embraces you and allows you, as a light being, or one who is created of the light, to have an experience. The love you hold within you is required for you to have experiences that you create for yourself. In other words, Source, or God, the creator who created you, was embraced by love in order to create. Now, you, God creator in your universe, must hold love for yourself. You must experience that sense of forgiveness, acceptance, and appreciation for yourself and others so that you, too, can create. These aspects are required for the love to hold the light, which brings about creation, the ignited spark, at any level of experience. (See also Source.)

Higher Self

Your higher self is your wiser self, rather than your personality. It is that part of you that incarnates partially into your world and remains partially in spirit. It bridges two worlds. It is you, but not all of you. When you access your intuition, you are accessing that part of you that is wise and brings you wisdom—your higher self—and beyond.

Your higher self is that part of your tube of light that is connected to Source and that is closest to your physical world. It is the lower portion of your tube, the portion of the tube that you can experience, that you can identify as your own. It is your personal experience of the tube when you exist in your physical reality.

Your higher self brings you information from Source by way of your intuition so that you may live a fuller life. It descends more or less into your awareness depending on your desire to connect to Source. It descends only so far, depending on your desire to receive information. You can choose whether or not to communicate with it.

You could say that your higher self is your access to higher wisdom. It is your intuition speaking to you through your tube of light. Remember, that "tube" is physically nonexistent, but you can imagine it as such to understand more easily what we are describing.

When you request something from Source, you are asking your higher self, or higher wisdom, the part of you that is incarnated, to access the subtler part of you that is less connected to this reality. That more subtle reality descends into your greater physical density through your higher self and brings you those experiences you desire.

Intuition

Simply stated, intuition is your access to Source, the Source of All That Is. Intuition is the aspect of you that descends as light particles in the column (which you could see as a beam or tube) of light to feed you information from Source. There must first be the request, because your intuition is set up to receive questions. These requests feed up the tube, so to say, as light particles through your higher self to your full self and on to Source. Source, or that grand being above you in creation, feeds back answers to your questions and requests. It is a feedback loop.

For example, you could see yourself raising your hand in class. When the teacher turns around from the blackboard, or whiteboard, he or she sees your hand and answers your question. There are times when you must wait for the teacher to turn around. When you receive your answer, you must make sense of it in your head. If you are not paying attention when the answer is given, you may hear only a portion of it. You could make mistakes in judgment if you applied only what you thought you heard because your interpretation of the answer would be incomplete. This is why it is useful to meditate and clear your mind. This allows you to hear the full answer you seek from the teacher.

When you receive your intuition, or answer, it is 100 percent up to you to apply it. If you are distracted or unsure of your desire, then the application of that intuition may be insufficient to move you ahead in a satisfactory manner. This is when you become upset with yourself. It is then time to clean out old patterns of existence and beliefs that hold you back from being pure and clean. If you do this, you will hear the answers more clearly. And having cleaned out the laziness in your system, you will apply your intuitions more thoroughly and be more satisfied with your results. Intuition:

- Is your communication device and the communication that contributes to your world by reminding you that you are God in your realm.
- Holds the pattern within it that lets you know you are nothing else but Source.
- Is meant to be activated and communicating with Source.
- Activates your world.
- Accompanies life force energy as an aspect of the light.
- Is information within the tube of light.

- Can be seen as light particles that hold wisdom.
- Is your knowing of who you are and how to be.
- Is information and acceptance of who you are as a whole being.
- Is your connection and access to Source.
- Is part of who you are.
- Can be present but not necessarily developed.
- Can be turned down, making the light appear dim.
- Can be reactivated after it has been forgotten and somewhat shut down.

Life Force Energy

Life force energy is the energy that comes down the tube of light with intuition to fill your body with light. It is on a mission from Source to ignite every cell in your body and bring your body life. This life force energy lodges itself in the nuclei of your cells. You could say that it is something like your DNA. This life force energy is information that is available to you at any time when you are ready to receive it. It is similar to intuition in that it feeds your body with life and all the answers you need at any time.

Intuition, you could say, feeds information to your subtler aspects, your more contemplative or mental aspects. But, truly, intuition and life force energy work together because intuition accesses information from your cells as well. It goes into your DNA and accesses information that is there. Intuition moves through your system seeking out answers, and some of the answers are held within your cells. Other answers are held within your energy around you. You can access information from universes within and without your being. But remember, as a whole being, you are truly one, and there is no difference between inside and out.

Light

Within the light is intuition and life force energy that feeds your body and mind with all the information you need to continue to grow and expand with every thought. Thoughts are of the light. They are of creation. When you hold love for yourself as you fill your body with light, you allow yourself to expand in the light even further. The goal is to have your physical body filled with light. (See also Tube of Light.) Light:

- Is created and held by love.
- Is a part of Source in this "outreach program" called life.
- Is your lifeline that connects you to Source.
- Wants to experience itself, so it transforms itself into creations.
- Ignites and activates your world.
- Contributes to your experiences by allowing you to have them.
- Holds the aspects of intuition and life force energy within it.
- Brings forth intuition and life force energy into your world
  so you can create.
- Is a connection that can be reestablished more fully if you
  forget that you are God. Without this connection, there is
  no reality.
- Delivers particles of information together in a "soup"
  specifically for you. It uses a contraption (tube, column,
  beam, stream) that is physically nonexistent.

Love

Love is the backdrop of all things. It is the petri dish to which you add the substance of light so that you may grow and evolve. It has no beginning and no end. It is the fabric, the deep velvetiness, or void, of space that holds love for you. It awaits your spark of light to enter its vastness, and then the further light that follows, to give birth to your experience. Love is:

- Older and wiser than Source.
- The original entity that created and received the light.
- The velvety material that receives light, appreciates it,
  and lets it grow and create in its realm.

- The expanse of space that allows creation to exist.
- The receptacle, or receiving device, within which light ignites form.
- The massive outlaying of potential.

Loving Yourself

The idea is to love yourself more. As you do so, your higher self, or that aspect of you that is wise and has access to Source, drops further into your reality and brings you more wisdom, more intuition. As this occurs, you experience more light moving throughout your whole system. You experience more life force energy flowing through you, which activates your cells. As this occurs, the nucleus of each entity or cell can give birth as well, and on and on it continues. As this occurs, you have access to more and more information.

This is why the expansion of the universe is so exciting. The more you expand, the more experiences you have. If you have been bored previously, you will not be bored as you expand yourself. It is truly the development of unfolding.

The more you love yourself, the more you forgive yourself and others for the past, the more you enjoy and appreciate who you are, the wider the expanse of love is within your system. This allows your light to expand. If you can love yourself more, you can double, triple or quadruple the available experiences for yourself because you have increased the container of love that can then receive more light, which, in turn, brings about even more experiences.

This is why focusing on loving yourself is the number one priority. Just as love came first in the universe, so is it for you in your universe. If you focus on love, loving yourself in your universe, appreciating who you are, forgiving yourself, and giving thanks for being love, you can then focus on creating. What do you desire? Once you know your desire, you ignite that spark of light and have an experience. If you decide you do not like that particular experience, you simply collapse the light in that area, move on, and create again. That is the microcosm and the macrocosm of creating.

Spark of Light

The spark of light within you welcomes the light that brings about life. It is the emanation of you that attracts you to the world. It waits in the fabric of love for more light to ignite it. You could say that "you" as a spark attract "you" as more light to your world.

It holds personal memories for you lodged behind your heart, so to say. This is why some say that when a person dies, the spark of light, or soul, leaves the heart area and moves on.

Your spark of light is held in love. It is the nucleus of your spirit. It has access to all of you. (See also Full Self.)

Source, Grander God

Source is the grand creator for your world. It is the expansiveness that is reaching out into the universe to experience itself. So, as your parent, let us say, Source guides you and allows you to have access to wisdom that is beyond your realm of experience. If you ask for help, Source is an available teacher for you. If you do not ask, nothing is offered. (See also God.) Source is:

- Born in love.
- The nucleus of the light.
- The center of your existence.
- The life-giving force that puts forth light.
- The creating device that goes out as light to experience itself as life.
- The beginning and ending of life.
- What you experience as the grand creator.
- The grander expression of who you are.
- Your parent. You are the children of Source, the children of the light held in love.
- Its own experience.

Tube of Light with Intuition and Life Force Energy

Even though you may envision it as light coming from Source in a contraption that we call a "tube," it is more specifically a beam, or a significant conglomeration of light, that is meant for you. The light has within it many aspects as it descends into your reality to bring life to you as the spark of light or soul. These many aspects work together in tandem to create your experience, or existence. This beam:

- Reaches you and gives you all the information you need in the way of intuition, life force energy, and connection to Source.
- Can be seen as a tube, column, or stream of light that retracts and extends.
- Is the contraption surrounding the light that does not have edges but is defined.

Wholeness

Wholeness is experienced through knowing you are God as that continuation of light from Source that has no beginning or end in your realm. When you are lacking intuition, you are lacking wholeness because you have eliminated an aspect of yourself that is due you.

To summarize, you are part of the whole that experiences your world as love and light. Source emanates light, and you are a spark of light. You are connected to Source through that tube of light, which holds intuition and life force energy within it. To fully function as a being, you must attribute goodness to yourself and experience yourself as part of Source held in love. Then your requests are instantaneously received through your intuition and you are able to receive back from Source the goodness of the universe.

About the Authors

Anne Salisbury and Greg Meyerhoff help clients find welcomed solutions to challenging situations so they can make decisions with confidence, ease, and joy. For people struggling with concerns around relationships and work, Anne and Greg hold the crystal ball. As professionally trained and conventionally educated consultants, workshop leaders, and speakers, they provide practical, easy to apply solutions that support profound transformations within their appreciative clients. They take clients from confusion to clarity, overwhelm to opportunity, and frustration to feeling good!

Anne Salisbury, PhD, ThD, MA, MBA is a clairvoyant seer who helps clients find answers to those important questions in life. She sees behind the veil to the meaning and purpose in life's problems. Anne has been involved in meditation, dreamwork, hypnotherapy, and intuitive skills development since the 1970s. She has met with the Dalai Lama and Mother Teresa in India. She holds advanced degrees in psychology, theology, and business and an undergraduate degree in art.

Greg Meyerhoff is an energy healer who breaks through the roadblocks in his clients' energy systems so they can experience success with ease. Through his unique abilities and techniques, he helps them achieve their health, romance, and work goals. Since 1975, Greg has studied and taught meditation and intuitive techniques. He has led dolphin encounters in the Caribbean. After receiving his degree in business management, Greg spent two decades as a senior account executive, where he honed his intuitive skills. For creating innovative solutions, he received the highest company awards.

In 1990, Anne founded the Transpersonal Hypnotherapy Institute, a Board of Education approved school that offers professional distance learning certification trainings in hypnosis and intuitive skills. THI has certified thousands of individuals in cutting edge techniques.

In 2000, Greg and Anne cofounded Intuitive Advantage, Inc. (that became Go Intuition, Inc.), which provides business consulting, intuitive counseling, energy clearing/feng shui, and pet psychic readings. They are based in Colorado and work worldwide with their many clients in person and by phone.

Together they developed the *Eureka System*™ which they teach in their trainings and talks. This is described in Anne's book, *Eureka! Understanding and Using the Power of Your Intuition.*

Visit *GoIntuition.com* and *TranspersonalInstitute.com* for more information.

Learn More ...

Speaking—Bring Intuition into Your Workplace or Organization

Anne Salisbury and Greg Meyerhoff are available for entertaining results-oriented speeches, seminars, and trainings on intuition.

Consulting—Receive Private Information

Anne and Greg provide business consulting, intuitive counseling, energy clearing/feng shui, and pet psychic readings in person and by phone. Where do you want your life and work life to be this time next year?

Distance Learning—Improve Your Intuition with Ease

Increase your ability to access intuition with comprehensive distance learning intuitive skills courses. Learn from the comfort of your home. Through listening to recordings of live classes and meaningful meditations for just a few minutes every day, you can achieve amazing results: decrease stress, increase focus, improve your decision making ability, and tap into your intuitive abilities.

Professional Training—Help Others Tap Into Their Intuition

Become a professional Certified Hypnotherapist through quality distance learning trainings. Watch DVDs of live classes and receive personal support while enrolled. The Transpersonal Hypnotherapy Institute, Inc. is approved by the Colorado Board of Education. Licensed Clinical Social Workers, Marriage and Family Therapists, Registered Nurses, and others can receive continuing education credits.

Please contact Anne F. Salisbury, PhD, and Greg Meyerhoff at
GoIntuition.com (main site)
TranspersonalInstitute.com (distance learning)

Bonus Gifts

Go Intuition eNewsletter

You can continue to be informed. Sign up to receive your free Go Intuition eNewsletter that focuses on how you can access your intuition. Each one embodies a nugget of truth that you can relate to immediately.

Visit *GoIntuition.com* to sign up for your free eNewsletter. You'll also find a host of free thought provoking articles there—click on Articles.

Free Audio Downloads

Download free audios of conversations with All That Is, as well as self-hypnosis scripts that can help you access your intuition. Make it easier on yourself to communicate with your intuitive wisdom.

Visit *GoIntuition.com* and click on Free Downloads.

Discover *Eureka!*

Eureka! Understanding and Using the Power of Your Intuition, by Anne Salisbury, PhD, is a valuable support for this book. It takes an analytical look at intuition and includes thought provoking exercises that you can apply immediately. In it you discover:

- What intuition is and is not
- How to tap into it
- How to trust it

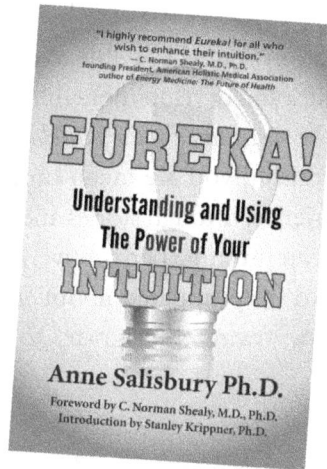

You come to understand the meaning behind this all-encompassing definition of intuition: "Intuition is the act or faculty of knowing immediately, directly and holistically without rational processes and without being aware of how you know. It is also the channel through which you access realms of universal truth, absolute knowledge and ultimate reality."

You delve into its history, the way it works in your life, what inhibits it and how techniques, such as meditation, self-hypnosis and dreamwork, encourage it. Everything you need to know about using your intuition is summed up in the easy-to-follow system of *ACT and LEAP™*. When applied, this can dramatically change your life:

Step 1: **A**sk for what you want
Step 2: **C**larify your desire
Step 3: Use **T**ools
Step 4: **L**et go
Step 5: **E**ureka!
Step 6: **A**ct on Eureka!
Step 7: **P**rove it

Visit *GoIntuition.com* or your local bookseller to order your copy today.

Coming Soon ...

Soon you will be able to discover new ways to increase your intuitive abilities and develop more fulfilling, enjoyable and successful relationships. In *The Intuition Factor in Relationships* by Anne Salisbury, PhD, and Greg Meyerhoff, you are taken on a journey into your heart where you can experience, through stories and exercises, what it is like to see relationships from an intuitive perspective.

To keep updated about *The Intuition Factor in Relationships*, visit *GoIntuition.com* to sign-up to receive your free eNewsletter.

www.ingramcontent.com/pod-product-compliance
Lightning Source LLC
Chambersburg PA
CBHW072132020426
42334CB00018B/1761